THE PREHISTORY OF WADI KUBBANIYA

Series assembled by
Fred Wendorf
and
Romuald Schild

Edited by
Angela E. Close

THE PREHISTORY OF WADI KUBBANIYA

Volume I

THE WADI KUBBANIYA SKELETON: A LATE PALEOLITHIC BURIAL FROM SOUTHERN EGYPT

by
Fred Wendorf
and
Romuald Schild

Edited by
Angela E. Close

Description of the Skeleton
by
T. D. Stewart
J. Lawrence Angel
Jennifer Olsen Kelley
and Michael Tiffany

Appendix by
Christopher L. Hill

SOUTHERN METHODIST UNIVERSITY PRESS • DALLAS • 1986

THE PREHISTORY OF WADI KUBBANIYA
VOLUME I, THE WADI KUBBANIYA SKELETON

CONTENTS

FOREWORD

During the course of an intensive study of several Late Paleolithic settlements in Wadi Kubbaniya, near Aswan in Egypt, a fossilized human skeleton was discovered, partially exposed on the surface and encased within a cemented block of calcareous sandstone. Our initial investigations suggested that the burial of the skeleton almost certainly preceded the earliest known Late Paleolithic settlements in the area and that it could well be contemporaneous with one of the late Middle Paleolithic occupations in the vicinity. This tentative conclusion concerning the age of the skeleton was reported to Dr. Ahmed Kadry, President of the Egyptian Antiquities Organization, together with a request that we be allowed to borrow the skeleton for one year. Dr. T. Dale Stewart, of the U.S. National Museum, is a physical anthropologist widely known for his work on the Shanidar Neanderthals; it was suggested that he would be the ideal person to direct the removal of the bones from their enclosing matrix and to conduct a technical study of them.

Dr. Kadry approved our request and a permit was issued for the skeleton to be transported to Washington. As part of this agreement, a final report on the skeleton was to be prepared and published separately. The agreement also stated that the skeleton should be removed from the enclosing matrix in such a way that a suitable exhibit concerning the discovery could be prepared, and that the skeleton should also be available for study by scholars in the future. These requirements were met by making a cast of the original block with the bones partially exposed, and also making casts of every bone after it had been removed from the matrix. The skeleton, the cast of the matrix block and the casts of the bones were returned to Egypt at the end of the one-year loan period.

We wish to express our thanks to Dr. Kadry and the staff of the Egyptian Antiquities Organization for their cooperation and support throughout this project. The transfer of human remains to a foreign country is always a highly emotional issue, and particularly so when those remains are regarded as among the oldest known from that country. We hope that the Antiquities Organization will view the results of our study, and the casts prepared for exhibit purposes, as justification of their confidence and trust. We also wish to thank the staff of the Foreign Currency Program at the Smithsonian Institution and the Anthropology Program of the National Science Foundation for financial support of the project on which the skeleton was discovered, and also for the additional funds needed to transport the skeleton to the United States. The Smithsonian Institution provided Grant FC80185500 and the National Science Foundation supported our work with Grant BNS8023411. We also wish to thank the staff of the Department of Vertebrate Paleontology at the U.S. National Museum for the assistance they gave to Dr. Stewart in removing the skeleton from the matrix block, and for the preparation of the superb casts of the block and the bones. Finally, we wish to thank Dr. Angela E. Close for the many hours she spent in editing this report. Although she has greatly improved the text and quality of the final product, she should not be held responsible for our observations and conclusions.

Fred Wendorf
Romuald Schild

CHAPTER 1

INTRODUCTION

by

Fred Wendorf and Romuald Schild

There are few areas in northeastern Africa, or, for that matter, anywhere in the Near East, where the Paleolithic remains have received such intensive study as that given to the Late Paleolithic settlements found in Wadi Kubbaniya. Wadi Kubbaniya is a major wadi which enters the Nile Valley from the west, a few kilometers north of Aswan, Egypt (Figure 1). Here, in 1978, test-excavations yielded four grains of barley and one grain of einkorn wheat, apparently in association with a buried hearth, from which charcoal was dated to 17,500 years ago. The presence of numerous grinding stones in that site and at several nearby sites of similar age suggested that cereals, whether wild or domestic, were being intensively utilized by the Late Paleolithic inhabitants of the area. If it were to be confirmed, it would have had a profound impact on our understanding of the origin of food-production and its role in the development of complex societies (Wendorf *et al.* 1979, 1980).

After the initial discovery of the cereals, four seasons of intensive excavation (1981–84) were carried out at Wadi Kubbaniya, in an effort to determine whether the cereals were in true association with the Late Paleolithic occupations and to obtain a better view of the internal structure of the sites, the settlement-pattern of which they were parts and the economic system represented in them. More cereals were found during these excavations, and it seemed very likely that we would have to make a major change in our traditional views of Late Paleolithic economies in the Nile Valley. Unfortunately (or fortunately, depending on one's point of view), our optimistic views concerning the precocious use of cereals had to be abandoned when the individual cereal grains were dated by the newly developed tandem linear accelerator, and the cereals were shown to be recent contaminations (Wendorf *et al.* 1984).

While this result was disappointing, our work at Wadi Kubbaniya has not been without considerable scientific benefit. It has given important new insights into the economy of the Late Paleolithic and has provided one of the most complete and detailed

records available from anywhere in the world on Late Paleolithic life-ways.

Another important scientific contribution of the work at Wadi Kubbaniya is the well-preserved, Late Paleolithic, human skeleton, which was found there during the 1982 season. The skeleton was discovered by the authors during routine survey and mapping activities near the mouth of the wadi (Figure 2). It was essentially a surface find, partially exposed by wind erosion. The body had been buried face down, probably in an extended position with head to the east and arms along the sides, in a pit dug into coarse aeolian sheet sands.

When first seen, the burial appeared as a sub-oval to sub-rectangular block of calcareous lithified sand with only the rear portions of the vertebrae, scapulae and pelvis exposed (Figures 3 and 4); the skull was not attached, the back portion of the calvarium was broken into numerous small pieces, and the face and mandible were still encased in a separate calcareous fragment which was broken vertically through the mandible and left orbit. Fragments of the skull, several foot-bones and other wind-rounded bone splinters littered the ground near the burial, particularly on the southern and southeastern sides. When the skeleton was first examined, it was believed that the legs might have been flexed and folded under the body. However, no legs were found when the matrix was removed in the laboratory. Subsequently, some of the rounded bone splinters found on the surface of the ground near the skeleton were identified as portions of the lower extremities. Apparently, the portion of the skeleton below the pelvis had been exposed earlier, the bones broken, either by the pressure of the earth, or perhaps by the hooves of passing animals, and the splinters then rounded by wind abrasion.

The remainder of the skeleton still encased in calcareous rock was cemented to the surrounding sediments by a mesh of small carbonaceous root-casts, which passed into the burial among the bones and beyond the pit into the surrounding coarse laminated sands. The cementation of the block

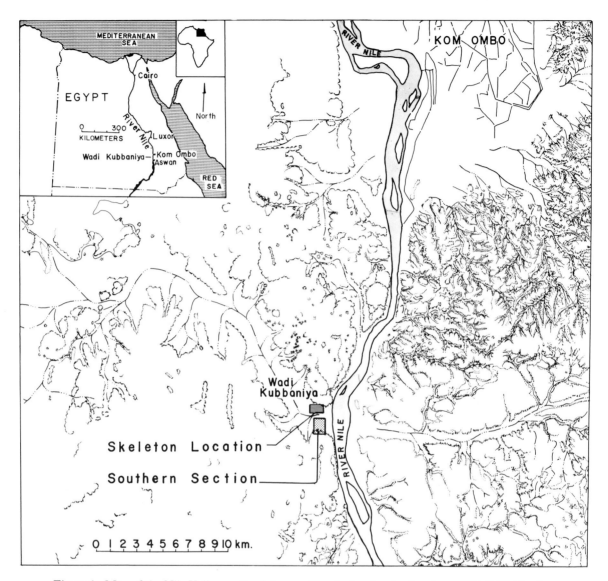

Figure 1. Map of the Nile Valley north of Aswan, Egypt, showing the location of Wadi Kubbaniya.

appeared to follow the shape of the grave-pit. The block is believed to be the result of calcium carbonate accumulation within the pit, and can be directly attributed to an abundance of lime-rich water percolating into the pit and to the difference in texture between the pit's loose fill of coarse gravelly sand and the relatively harder, laminated sands into which it had been cut.

In so far as could be determined, the fill of the burial pit consisted entirely of the same coarse sands as surrounded the pit, except, of course, that they were no longer laminated. Significantly, there were no traces of the Nilotic silt which lies directly over

the coarse, laminated sand only a few meters away, and which at one time undoubtedly covered the burial pit. Since it would be impossible to excavate a pit through a thick layer of fine, powdery silt into the coarse sand, and then to refill the pit with coarse sand only (unless a conscious effort were made to exclude the silt, and even then it would be extremely difficult), the excavation of the burial-pit must have been made prior to the deposition of the Nile silt over the area of the burial, or after the removal of the silt by erosion and deflation. There is strong evidence to suggest that the first is the more likely explanation.

Figure 2. View of Wadi Kubbaniya, looking south across the area of Middle Paleolithic finds near the wadi mouth.

Another indication of antiquity was the highly mineralized character of the skeleton, which contrasted strongly with the only slightly mineralized fish and mammal bones at two nearby Late Paleolithic settlements, associated with the Late Paleolithic silts which cover much of the area. These settlements are dated by radiocarbon to about 20,000 years ago, so that a much greater antiquity was suggested for the skeleton.

Initially, we thought that the skeleton might be of Middle Paleolithic age. A concentration of Middle Paleolithic artifacts occurred nearby, embedded in the underlying silt units, and many lithic artifacts of Mousteroid character were found *in situ* within the coarse laminated sands below the skeleton and even possibly stratigraphically above it where the upper part of the sands was preserved on an adjacent knoll. Thus, when the burial block was being removed, it seemed highly likely that the skeleton might be that of an individual who had died during the period when the later part of the laminated sand sheet was being deposited. If so, the skeleton would be of late Middle Paleolithic age.

When the calcareous lithified sand was cut from around the skeleton, however, two bladelets were found in the left abdominal region, between the lowermost ribs and the lumbar vertebrae. These bladelets are technologically and typologically of Late Paleolithic character, and are not likely to be Middle Paleolithic in age. The skeleton is therefore probably associated with the Late Paleolithic and dates to some time prior to the deposition of the Nile silts which cover the coarse laminated sands in the area, or before 20,000 years ago, but after the development of bladelet technology.

THE KUBBANIYA AREA

Wadi Kubbaniya is one of three major drainages which come into the Nile from the southwestern desert (Figure 1). It joins the Nile about 12 km north of Aswan and is the most important wadi on the west bank of the Nile from southwest of Aswan to Luxor. It drains most of the area between the river and the Sinn el Kaddab scarp of the Eocene plateau on the west. Today it is dry and discharges water into the Nile only very rarely—after unusually heavy rains such as have fallen perhaps only once or twice during the past century.

Figure 3. View of burial block as first discovered.

The wadi enters the Nile Valley from the northwest through a narrow gorge located just opposite Wadi Abu Subeira, which is a large, deep course draining the northeastern portion of the Red Sea Hills. Both are structural features. The Nile Valley from Aswan northward to a few kilometers beyond Kubbaniya is the narrowest section of Valley in Egypt. It ranges between 1000 and 2000 m in width and is bordered on both sides by steep Nubia sandstone cliffs. The two opposed wadi mouths of Abu Subeira and Kubbaniya form the widest plain between Aswan and Kom Ombo, some 30 km to the north. The modern village of Kubbaniya lies on recent wash sediments and late Middle Paleolithic Nilotic silts at the very mouth of the wadi. The adjacent, narrow floodplain is at an elevation of *ca.* 90–91 m above sea level.

Near its mouth Wadi Kubbaniya is bounded on both the north and south sides by nearly vertical scarps of Nubia sandstone, which stand from 30 to 50 m above the floor of the wadi. Sand and gravel remnants of older wadi aggradations are preserved as terraces in several areas, particularly in the lower portion of the wadi.

Most of the Late Paleolithic sites in Wadi Kubbaniya occur embedded in a massive remnant of dune sand and interfingering silt located about three kilometers up the wadi from its mouth. Excavations in this dune/silt remnant indicated that it accumulated when the Nile had filled its channel and was flowing at a higher level than that of today (about 8–10 m above the modern floodplain). During seasonal floods, the Nile waters entered the wadi for a distance of several kilometers and permitted vegetation to grow along the edge of the floodplain. The surrounding desert was hyperarid and northerly winds moved sand from the adjacent, barren sandstone uplands down into the wadi, where it was trapped by the vegetation and built extensive dunefields close to the northern scarp.

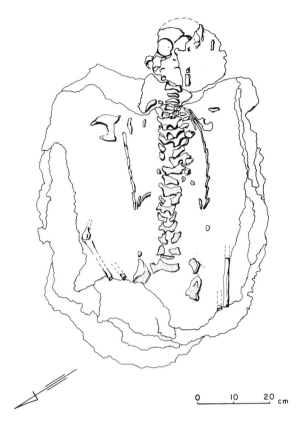

0   10   20 cm

Figure 4. Sketch plan of the skeleton as first observed.

The seasonal floods would cover the lower parts of these dunes and leave a thin lens of silt. When the flood water receded, another layer of sand would be deposited over the silt, resulting in a rhythmical pattern of alternating dune and silt accumulation.

Meanwhile, the center of the wadi became a flood-plain with gradually accumulating lenses of silt. Fish were brought into the wadi with the flood waters and, when the flood level fell, many of these fish were trapped in the numerous pools and swales within the dune field and adjacent floodplain. The fish were a major attraction for Late Paleolithic people, who repeatedly camped on the dunes and collected and cooked the fish.

Near the mouth of Wadi Kubbaniya, against the northern scarp, is another, smaller remnant of alternating sands and silts, that fill a small basin cut into earlier wadi gravels. This small remnant also contains Late Paleolithic sites with lithic assemblages similar to those from the earliest sites known in the dune field farther up the wadi, and with associated radiocarbon dates on charcoal of about the same age—18,500 to 21,000 B.P. The artifacts in these earliest sites differ slightly from those in sites dating between 18,500 and 17,000 B.P. (which we have named the Kubbaniyan), but it is not clear whether these earlier sites should be called "Early Kubbaniyan" or whether they should be given a separate name. "Early Kubbaniyan" will be used here for ease of reference.

The dune/silt layers near the mouth of the wadi, in which the Early Kubbaniyan sites occur, lie over yet another series of interfingering aeolian and fluviatile sediments. A major unconformity separates the two suites of sand and silt accumulation, but both seem to reflect the same complex processes operating at two very different times in the past. The lower suite contains several small clusters of Mousteroid artifacts and is believed to be of late Middle Paleolithic age. It rests directly on the eroded surface of still older wadi deposits, into which the small basin had been cut.

CHAPTER 2

THE GEOLOGICAL SETTING

by

Romuald Schild and Fred Wendorf

PRE-PLEISTOCENE AND EARLY PLEISTOCENE SEDIMENTS

Wadi Kubbaniya is the northernmost of the three wadis which cross the western Kalabsha Plain (Figure 5), a well developed Nubia sandstone pediplain, 30–50 km west of the Nile, extending from the Gallaba Gravel Plain in the north to the latitude of Dakka in the south (Butzer and Hansen 1968:213). The Kalabsha pediplain is a monotonous, sandstone surface, dotted with isolated sandstone hillocks. It has an elevation of 180–210 m above sea-level and is characterized by undulating relief and rather poor and shallow drainage.

The head of Wadi Kubbaniya reaches almost to the Sinn el Kaddab scarp of the limestone plateau in the west, passing, in shallow drainage channels, through the Muneih and Kurkur Forelands (Butzer and Hansen 1968:30), a rough, grey, stony surface of the Dakhla Formation. The lower, eastern portion of Wadi Kubbaniya follows two complex fractures striking at N33°W and N43°W and, in the Nile Valley, it joins the fault of Wadi Abu Subeira which has a strike of N85°W (Butzer and Hansen 1968:27). The wadi enters the Nile Valley from the northwest through a narrow gorge just opposite Wadi Abu Subeira, which is a large, deep course draining the northeastern portion of the Kalabsha Plain and the western Etbai Uplands of the Nubian Desert (Figure 1).

Most of the middle and lower course of Wadi Kubbaniya is cut into Nubia Sandstone overlain by a characteristic bed of variable thickness, made up of silts, coarse sand, gravel, pebbles and boulders. These obviously riverine sands and gravels, composed mainly of quartz with some admixture of igneous and metamorphic rocks, have long attracted the attention of geologists working along the Nile. They were observed by Passarge in 1914 (Blank and Passarge 1925) and later by Uhden (1929) in the area of the First Cataract. Said (1962:91) mentions them in his earlier work as being present on the left bank of the river near the Kom Ombo Plain.

However, only Chumakov (1967), followed by Butzer and Hansen (1968) and by the later teams of the Geological Survey of Egypt (Said 1975, 1981; Issawi and Hinnawi 1980; Issawi 1983), have spent considerable time studying them in detail.

According to Chumakov (1967), the more or less discontinuous bed of sand and gravel occurs primarily on the left bank between Kom Ombo and Aswan, with isolated patches located near Wadi Halfa (Chumakov 1967:58–59). The absolute elevations of the gravels in the area of Kom Ombo are in the range of 150–160 m above sea-level, while some of the caprock patches near Aswan may be slightly more than 200 m above sea-level. To the north of Aswan, the gravel beds form a huge plain which slopes gently northwards. Trenches, outcrops and bore-holes associated with the construction of the Aswan–Cairo power-line enabled Chumakov to obtain data concerning the composition and structure of these sediments (1967:57–58). The sand and gravel bed seems to be composed of two distinct series. The upper one, 2–3 m in thickness, is made up of red gravels, pebbles and cobbles in a coarse sand matrix. The pebbles, gravels and cobbles are well rounded and are mostly quartz and quartzite with some weathered igneous and metamorphic rocks. In places, the upper 3–5 m of the sediments do not contain any sand, but the amount of sand usually increases downward while the coarser material diminishes. At 2.5–3 m below the surface, the sediment is made up of grey and reddish brown sands containing 5–25% gravel and pebbles. The sands are horizontally or obliquely bedded and are often well sorted. The maximal depth reached in the lower series was 8–10 m, although its total thickness appears to have been about 30 m and it could have been even thicker in areas where the sands filled earlier concavities and fossil wadis (Chumakov 1967:58).

Chumakov (1967) introduced the formal name of Kubbaniya Series (or Suite) for these sands and gravels, following his major effort which was concentrated in the middle course of Wadi Kubbaniya.

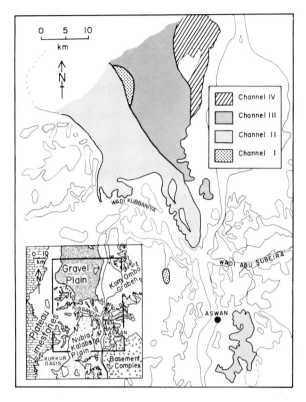

Figure 5. Geological map of the area west of Kom Ombo showing the distribution of the deposits identified with four old river channels.

The Kubbaniya Series, according to Chumakov, formed the last, alluvial section of the three Pliocene series, although it had been deposited by the pre-Nile during the Villafranchian (Chumakov 1967:66).

Butzer and Hansen assigned an important role to Wadi Kubbaniya in the Late Pliocene and Early Pleistocene history of the Nile. They believed that during the Upper Pliocene "major discharge of the Nubian Nile may have been channeled through what is today called Wadi-el-Kubbaniya" (1968: 43), a water course combining the discharge of Wadi Kharit and flowing through Wadi Abu Subeira to empty into the Kom Ombo salt lake. A diminished role is envisaged for the Wadis Kharit, Abu Subeira and Kubbaniya drainage system in the deposition of the Gallaba Gravel Plain during the Early Pleistocene. This huge expanse of gravels

extends along the Darb el Gallaba caravan trail on the left bank of the river at an elevation of *ca.* 150–160 m above sea-level (Butzer and Hansen 1968: 44) and seems to merge into gravel beds of the Kubbaniya suite of Chumakov. The major discharge responsible for the deposition of the Darb el Gallaba gravels, however, is associated by Butzer and Hansen (1968:45) with the Wadis Shait, Hatash and Kharit-Abu Subeira system of the Nubian Desert. On the basis of unspecified benches along Wadi Kubbaniya, they infer a width of 5 km for the Nile flowing through the wadi.

The studies of Chumakov were known to Butzer and Hansen from correspondence and from an early summary published in 1965 (Chumakov 1965). Because of the difference in elevation, they believed that the Kubbaniya Series of Chumakov was older than the Gallaba gravels and should be placed in the Basal Pleistocene rather than in the Early Pleistocene as Chumakov suggested (Butzer and Hansen 1968:42). Recent summaries of the history of the Nile by Said (1975, 1981) give yet another interpretation of the Kubbaniya and Gallaba gravels. Taking into consideration both the lithology and the stratigraphy of the gravels, Said believes that this huge expanse of deposits extends along the west bank from Wadi Kubbaniya in the south to El Sibaiya in the north with a few isolated patches farther south in Nubia, as noted by Giegengack (1968). Said assigns the formal name of Idfu Formation to these gravels (1975:21), and states that they are mineralogically different from the gravels of eastern Kom Ombo. The Idfu complex of sand and gravels is interpreted as the deposit of a braided river of Early Pleistocene age "capable of transporting cobble-size gravels for long distances" (Said 1975:23).

This brief review of the several interpretations of the Kubbaniya and Kom Ombo gravels indicates that research is still only at a preliminary stage. The work of Issawi and Hinnawi (1980) at Wadi Kubbaniya and adjacent areas (Issawi *et al.* 1978; Issawi 1983) presents many new data and indicates that the problems involved are of considerable complexity. Several river channels have been recorded at different elevations. It is believed that the channels represent rivers of Plio-Pleistocene age draining the Red Sea Hills, and they have been named the Kom Ombo gravels. These latest discoveries are shown in Figures 5 and 6, by Issawi.

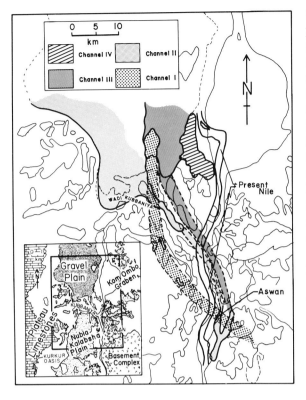

Figure 6. Map of probable location of old channels.

Late Pleistocene Sediments in the Mouth of Wadi Kubbaniya

The Geological Model

The geomorphological setting of Wadi Kubbaniya, with its high scarps, the narrow Nile Valley and considerable protection from northerly winds, is responsible for the excellent preservation of the Late Pleistocene sediments in its mouth, particularly in the lowermost 4 km of the wadi. This is also the area where the Nile waters could enter the wadi and deposit alluvial and lacustrine sediments. The wadi itself was not active during the periods of Nilotic accumulation, so that the sediments remained undisturbed throughout most of the Late Pleistocene.

Only during the last of the Early Holocene wet periods did renewed wadi activity result in the cutting of a deep Holocene channel through the central section of the older Nilotic and aeolian suites. The renewed deflation of the succeeding hyper-arid period then considerably reduced the older deposits. As a result, only two main sections of Late Pleistocene alluvial and aeolian sediments remain relatively undisturbed. The larger one is on the north side of the wadi extending up to the first major tributary wadi, and is referred to below as the Northern Section; the smaller one is along the footslopes of the southern cliff in the wadi mouth and is referred to below as the Southern Section. Several discontinuous remnants of Nilotic, lacustrine and associated aeolian deposits occur as very reduced patches of older sediments among later deposits. These extend along the southeastern footslopes of the cliffs and the edge of the latest wadi channel.

Our initial work at Wadi Kubbaniya soon showed that the area was not only rich in archaeological occurrences but was also extremely promising as a key locality for the study of the Late Pleistocene behavior of the river and surrounding desert. The complexity of the sediments, their thickness, their obvious association with human settlements and the good preservation of organic remains were unique in the whole Egyptian and Nubian Nile Valley. Detailed geomorphological studies could be expected to lead to an unusually complete picture of the environment exploited by prehistoric man in Wadi Kubbaniya.

There has been a diversity of opinion concerning the lithostratigraphy and behavior of the Late Pleistocene Nile (Butzer and Hansen 1968; de Heinzelin 1968; Wendorf and Schild 1976; Butzer 1980; Said 1981). In spite of the differences, however, several beliefs are common to these earlier studies: that the permanent link of the Nile with its modern headwaters was not established before the beginning of Late Paleolithic as it was then understood; that there were several aggradations resulting from increases in river discharge, flow and competence; and that the aggradations were separated by recessions caused by reduced Nilotic flow and discharge, during which periods dune sands invaded the valley floor from the adjacent desert.

Butzer and Hansen (1968), Butzer (1980) and de Heinzelin (1968) each recognized three aggradational events and several minor ones in the Late

Pleistocene and Early Holocene, but they differed significantly concerning the chronology of these events. Wendorf and Schild (1976), employing new data from Upper Egypt and the Fayum, attempted to reconcile the differences, but still followed the general framework established during the Nubian Campaign by Butzer, Hansen and de Heinzelin. Eventually, however, it was realized that there were two areas of radical difficulty with this framework. The first arose from the dating and differentiation of the various units recognized by the framework, and the second, more basic, concerned the geomorphological model itself.

An early indication of significant inconsistency within all of the proposed schemes was given when a group of radiocarbon dates was rerun for the archaeological sites associated with the oldest of the supposed Late Pleistocene aggradations (Wendorf *et al.* 1979). These sites were assigned to the Khormusan industry, and occurred in Nilotic sediments 11–28 m above the modern floodplain in Sudanese Nubia. The Khormusan had been believed to be Late Paleolithic (Marks 1968), but the reprocessed samples showed that some of the sites were more than 41,490 years old (SMU-107, from Site 34D), and even the youngest of them appears to be beyond the range of the radiocarbon technique (Site 6G30 [Irwin *et al.* 1968] has a date of >36,000 B.P.). The Khormusan is therefore Middle Paleolithic in age (specifically late Middle Paleolithic), as must also be the sediments in which it occurs. These sediments are Nilotic sediments, of Ethiopian or equatorial origin, found at much higher elevations than the modern floodplain.

The next-oldest series of Paleolithic sites known to be associated with a Nilotic floodplain much higher than that of today are typically Late Paleolithic. Several taxonomic entities are recognized and they are firmly dated by numerous radiocarbon dates. The oldest of them are slightly more than 20,000 years old, both in Sudanese Nubia at Site 6B32 (Irwin *et al.* 1968) and in Wadi Kubbaniya (Sites E-81-4, E-82-3 and E-81-6). In most cases, however, late Middle Paleolithic and Late Paleolithic deposits (both Nilotic and associated aeolian and lacustrine sediments) are indistinguishable in the field, both in appearance and in elevation. Further, laboratory analyses of heavy minerals have shown no significant differences between silt samples ascribed to them. They may eventually prove to

be distinguishable, but that still needs considerable testing (Butzer and Hansen 1968; Hassan 1976a, 1976b). The formational names introduced for the Nilotic and associated sediments are therefore misleading, since the lithological components of the various formations cannot be differentiated in the field. The faunas included within the sediments of both Middle and Late Paleolithic age are identical, so that, at present, only the cultural components and absolute dating can clarify the lithostratigraphic and chronological complexities of the Late Pleistocene Nile Valley.

More basic than this, however, is the problem of the underlying model of the behavior of the Nile during the Late Pleistocene and of the very existence of the "aggradations" and "recessions". The original explanation, that aggradations resulted from greater Ethiopian and equatorial discharge, does not fit the data gathered along the Blue and White Niles where, it seems, there was actually a much lower discharge at the time of the Nilotic Late Paleolithic "aggradation" (Williams and Adamson 1974; Gasse and Street 1979; Street and Grove 1979; Harvey 1976; Gasse 1976; Kendall 1969). Furthermore, the level of the Mediterranean Sea was much lower during the Last Glaciation, particularly around the glacial maximum at slightly before 20,000 B.P. A very low base level and a highly competent river would have resulted in rapid downcutting.

The original model, that the Late Pleistocene Nile was a competent, powerful river with high precipitation in its headwaters, is contradicted by the available data and has therefore been rejected (Schild and Wendorf 1980:45). Instead, it has been proposed that there was less rain over the northwestern portion of the Ethiopian Plateau, that the rainy season was shorter and that the total discharge of the Nile was much less. The so-called "aggradations", which occurred during periods of lowered base levels, resulted from the greatly increased accumulation of sediments within an intensively braided, shallow and highly seasonal river (Schild and Wendorf 1980:45). The river was of reduced competence, but still of considerable seasonal capacity and sediment load, which led to a steady rise of the floodplain and its braided channels. This hypothesis is corroborated by the restricted faunal spectra found in Late Pleistocene sites along the main Nile, indicating that the carrying-capacity of the valley was limited. A very similar hypothesis has recently been put forward by Adamson and others (Adamson 1982; Adamson *et al.* 1982).

The testing of this hypothesis required further field-work at carefully selected areas. Wadi Kubbaniya, with its potential for absolute dating and its manageable area of well-preserved sediments, seemed to be one of the most promising of such areas. The field-work design for Wadi Kubbaniya included very detailed geological mapping, accompanied by intensive trenching and coring. All of the recognized units were to be physically connected and their stratigraphic relationships established. A number of long, composite cross-sections would show the stratigraphic setting in every area. A contour map was to be drawn to the same scale as the lithological one, with a contour-interval of 1 m. A number of sedimentological analyses were also planned.

Most of the planned field studies in Wadi Kubbaniya were completed. The detailed lithological and contour maps were made (Figure 7). Extensive lithostratigraphic data were gathered at the numerous cuts and trenches, which were dug at every excavated site (Figure 8). Additionally, there were 115 stratigraphic trenches and 37 bore-holes, some to a depth of almost 7 m. Other data were obtained from the 37 soundings made at the corners of the 200-m. grid and from the 88 smaller soundings which were dug in the main portion of the so-called floodplain area of the Northern Section. More than ten composite cross-sections, some covering more than 1000 m, were prepared to show the exact stratigraphic setting of the Wadi Kubbaniya sequence. Chronological placement of the units was secured by 52 radiocarbon dates, two thermoluminescence dates and one uranium/thorium date.

Earlier Late Pleistocene Sediments

The geological work in Wadi Kubbaniya was concentrated at the mouth of the wadi, on sediments deposited by the Nile or interbedded with such deposits. The detailed geological mapping, preparation of the general cross-sections and work at the Aterian site of E-78-11 yielded some information concerning the complex Pleistocene geological history of the wadi, but our data on these earlier episodes are generally poor.

Surficial observations of the earlier sediments, upstream from the areas of study, indicate that there are probably at least four gravel terraces along the northern bank, with numerous wind-abraded Early and Middle Paleolithic artifacts occurring on their surfaces. The terraces are all highly dissected and are composed of gravels and cobbles derived primarily from the Kom Ombo gravels (Issawi and Hinnawi 1980; Issawi 1983; Issawi *et al.* 1978). The oldest terrace lies just below the gravel-sandstone plain at an elevation of slightly more than 150 m asl and is capped by a deep red soil. Immediately to the north of the northern Nilotic remnant, the terraces are dissected by tributary wadis, or have been removed and replaced by various slope washes and tributary wadi deposits which fan into the main wadi bed.

On the southern bank, opposite the main area of Nilotic sediments, is an extensive and eroded sandy terrace which is heavily masked by Late Pleistocene dunes and recent slope wash. There are extensive exposures of this terrace along the right bank of the Holocene channel. Its elevation ranges at least between *ca.* 103 m asl (the base was not reached) and 113 m asl (at what might be the top). A scatter of aeolized, redeposited Aterian artifacts (Site E-78-11) was collected from the surface of the terrace (Singleton and Close 1980). The terrace is made up of white (5Y 8/2) to pale yellow (2.5Y 8/4), coarse and medium-grained, rather poorly sorted sand with occasional well-rounded pebbles. A thin bed of similar pebbles is included within the terrace. The sands are heavily cemented and impenetrable by pick, and there are secondary gley reduction and enrichment zones near the base. Laterally and upslope, the white terrace sands seem to grade into pale brown slope (?) sands with large vertical jointings. The bedding is usually masked by secondary enrichments in calcium carbonate. Downstream, the terrace is dissected by a large tributary wadi and masked by later deposits. This white, heavily cemented, sandy terrace is a fragment of old wadi deposits which predate not only the Late Pleistocene riverine, lacustrine and aeolian complexes, but also the slope and wadi sediments immediately underlying them.

Along the northern fringes of the Northern Section of the Nilotic and aeolian complex is a series of wadi and slope deposits, seen in deflational windows or exposed by the Holocene alluvial activity of

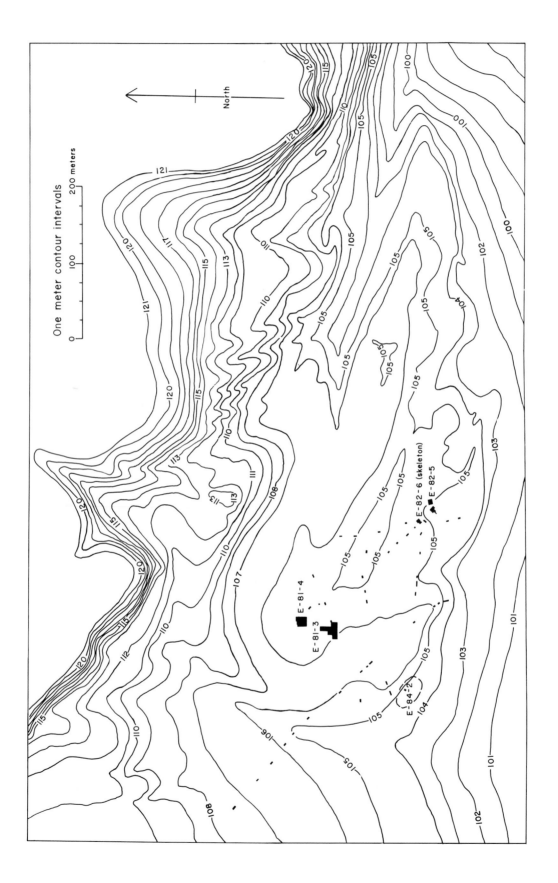

Figure 7. Contour map of the Middle Paleolithic Area near the mouth of Wadi Kubbaniya. Elevations in m asl. Map prepared by Ali Mazhar, Geological Survey of Egypt.

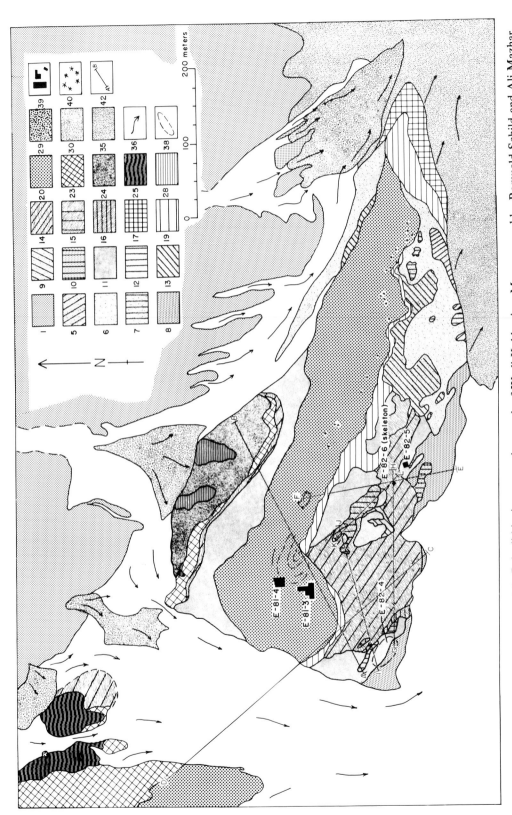

Figure 8. Geological map of the Middle Paleolithic Area near the mouth of Wadi Kubbaniya. Map prepared by Romuald Schild and Ali Mazhar.

KEY: 1–Nubia sandstone. *Middle Paleolithic Nilotic and Aeolian Sediments:* 5–middle basin silt; 6–middle dune; 7–middle dune crust; 8–floodplain silt; 9–upper basin silt; 10–sandy basin within floodplain silt; 11–upper dune; 12–upper dune crust; 13–lower stabilization zone; 14–sand sheet; 15–sand sheet crusts; 16–upper stabilization zone; 17–channel sands and silts. *Late Paleolithic Sediments:* 19–lower Kubbaniyan silt; 20–lower Kubbaniyan dune; 23–middle Kubbaniyan silt; 24–upper Kubbaniyan dune; 25–upper lacustrine series. *Holocene Sediments:* 28–Early Holocene alluvial cone; 29–Holocene slope wash; 30–alluvial core coarse; 35–fine late wash; 36–modern wadi wash. *Other:* 38–limit of lithic artifact concentration; 39–area of site excavations; 40–fossil vegetation casts; 42–profile lines.

a tributary wadi joining the main course from the nearby embayment. This recent wadi activity has largely destroyed or masked the earlier sediments of similar origin. A coarse slope wash, with sub-rounded to rounded gravel and pebbles in a sandy matrix, is believed to be the oldest bed in this section. It is overlain by a fine, powdery slope wash with occasional gravel, which disappears under the adjacent dune field. A small remnant of a gravely wadi terrace caps the sequence of wadi and slope deposits. This terrace reaches an elevation of *ca.* 109 m asl, and has large Levallois flakes on its surface, which have been wind-abraded but not rolled.

These alluvial and slope sediments precede the deposition of Nilotic silts and associated dunes. All of the deep cores, sunk through the Nilotic and aeolian sediments in this section of the wadi, reach wadi gravels apparently of the same episode at elevations of *ca.* 101–102 m asl. Farther down the wadi, in the eastern part of the Northern Section, the top of the alluvial deposits under the Nilotic complex ranges from *ca.* 97 m to 101 m asl, depending on local morphology, while the slope deposits are between *ca.* 101 m and 103 m asl. In the Southern Section, the underlying wadi gravels are at *ca.* 101 m asl. The wadi gravels were exposed in trenches only in the northern part of the Northern Section. In Pit A/4, the bed is 2 m below the surface and under the Late Paleolithic aeolian sand of the main dune field. The gravels and pebbles are well rounded and heavily cemented. In the central part of the Northern Section the gravels occur at least 4 m below the surface, while in the eastern part of the Northern Section and in the Southern Section they are 6–7 m below the Middle Paleolithic silts and related beds.

The gravels always underlie the first traces of Nilotic deposits and never interfinger with them, neither are they interbedded with the silts, aeolian sands or lacustrine beds. This is in accord with other Nilotic or related deposits. Extensive work in the Western Desert of Egypt (Wendorf and Schild 1980) has shown that the desert was hyperarid during the Late Pleistocene (except for the earliest part, contemporaneous with the early Middle Paleolithic and, perhaps, the Last Interglacial). Very similar data are available from the central and western Sahara, except for the high lacustrine stands of Lake Chad, Erg Chech, Ahnet-Mouydir and Sebkha Chemchane. All of these are radio-carbon-dated to about 20,000 B.P. but the radio-carbon dates are on carbonates and should, there-fore, be viewed with some reservation (van Zin-deren Bakker 1972; Rognon and Williams 1977; Rognon 1980; Beaudet *et al.* 1976).

The Middle Paleolithic Valley Filling Episode

The morphology of the eastern part of the Northern Section, prior to the earliest recorded accumulation of Nilotic silts, has been reconstructed on the basis of many bore holes. Most of the silts lie in a clear trough cut into the Nubia Sandstone and partially filled with wadi and slope deposits. A Nubia Sand-stone ridge in the southeastern portion of the North-ern Section, oriented northwest–southeast, suggests that the first Nilotic sediments were deposited in the mouth of a small tributary wadi descending from the scarp in the same place where one exists today (Figures 11–13); the sandstone ridge would form the right bank of this wadi (Figure 9). Another fossil tributary wadi, although shallow, was recorded below the recent one which separates the eastern and western areas of the Northern Section (Figure 10). Channels of modern and Holocene tributary wadis tend to reexcavate the fossil channels because of the similar morphology of the scarps.

Almost 7 m of Nilotic and aeolian sediments overlie the Nubia Sandstone (Figure 10:1) and wadi or slope deposits (Figure 10:2 and 2a) in the eastern part of the Northern Section; most of these are associated with the Middle Paleolithic filling of the Nile Valley. Pre-existing morphology was responsi-ble for some of the facial features both in the fossil tributary wadi and elsewhere in the mouth of Wadi Kubbaniya. In the tributary wadi trough, Nilotic deposition took place in a small sheltered bay which was being invaded by dunes descending from the adjacent scarp. The bay was soon closed by the dunes, and the later silts were laid down in a closed basin, whose general features are still visible today.

Deposition in the basin took place throughout most of the Middle Paleolithic filling of the Nile Valley and at the beginning of the Late Paleolithic one. Outside the bay, the areas close to the Nile received fine alluvial sands and silts of the channel marginal zone, while typical floodplain silts and clays are the only sediments farther inside the mouth of Wadi Kubbaniya.

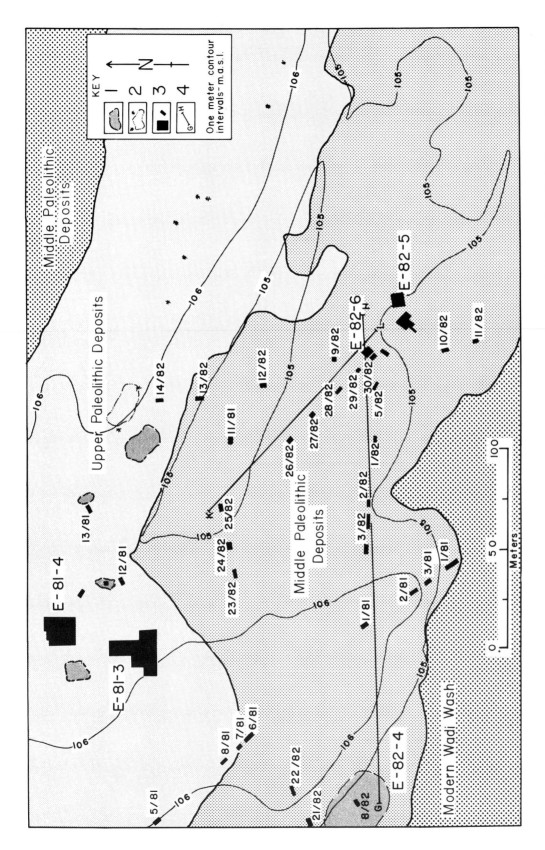

Figure 9. Map of Middle Paleolithic Area near the mouth of Wadi Kubbaniya showing the positions of all excavations, including trenches, and their relationship to the Middle Paleolithic, Late Paleolithic and modern wadi sedimentary groups. KEY: 1–Artifact concentrations on surface; 2–cluster of fossil vegetation—probably deflated remnant of a phytogenic dune; 3–excavated areas and trenches; 4–lines of profiles. Map prepared by Ali Mazhar.

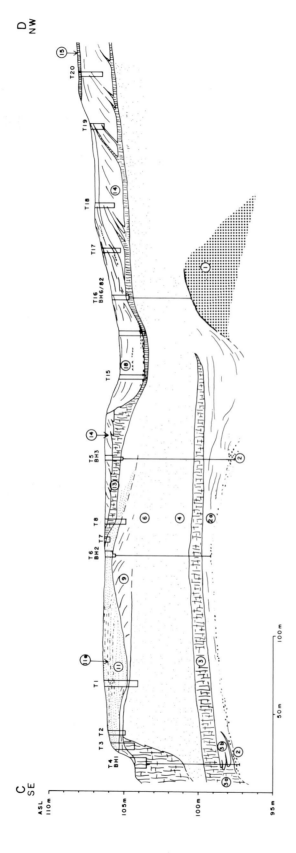

Figure 10. Cross-section C–D.

Key

1—Nubia sandstone, base of coring when not covered by gravel.

2—Rounded to semi-rounded gravel of quartz and igneous rocks with some local sandstone gravel increasing in amount toward scarp; sandstone gravel sub-rounded to rounded in bore holes close to scarp. Matrix is formed by loose, coarse, unsorted sand, sometimes friable, very pale brown (10YR 7/4) or yellowish brown (10YR 6/4) in color—wadi and slope alluvial wash, grading up into friable to loose, coarse, unsorted sand of possible aeolian or mixed aeolian and alluvial origin (2a), bedding inferred.

3—*Lower Basin Silt*—dark brown (10YR 4/2 to 7.5YR 4/2) clay with slickensides and small blocky structure, cemented to consolidated, deposited in basin formed by wadi cut. Laterally, toward southeast and center of main wadi, seems to grade into floodplain silt (3a) with a shore zone with reworked sand lenses (3b). In northwestern

section of basin, several sand lenses, either shore-wash or inblown dune sand, observed within bed (3c). Lower Basin Silt known only from bore holes and, thus, its microstratigraphic relationship to massive floodplain silt unknown. Probably forms a lower part of seemingly homogeneous floodplain silt in areas beyond basin.

4—*Lower Dune*—light yellowish brown (10YR 6/4) dune sand highly cemented at top, grading down into consolidated, very pale brown (10YR 7/4), aeolian sand. Base friable to loose, coarse sand, possibly a sand sheet with original desert coloring (4a). Sand seems to grade laterally (toward center of basin) into light yellowish (10YR 6/4), friable, unsorted sand with dark brown (7.5YR 4/2) silt lenses (4b), an apparently early phase of next siltation contemporaneous with deposition of sand bed. Because of 4a, it is inferred that middle basin silt is largely contemporaneous with deposition of sand bed and, therefore, they should interfinger. In southeastern section of basin

(Figure 11), Lower Dune is clearly separated from Middle Dune or Yellow Dune, by a bed of basin silt (5). Along southwestern bank of basin, in area where Middle Basin Silt is not present, two dunes are not separated in bore holes. Main body of Lower Dune obviously deposited along southwestern bank of basin.

5—*Middle Basin Silt*—highly cemented, pale brown (10YR 6/3), highly calcareous silt with a calcareous, light brownish grey (2.5Y 6/2) crust at topmost 10 cm in center of basin. In thickest portion, in center of basin, and in its southeastern section, lower portion of silt dark brown (7.5YR 4/2) with small blocky structure and less calcareous. This silt outcrops on surface at very edge of complex, in its southeastern section where its top seems to be slightly higher than in fossil wadi basin. Not observed along southwestern bank of basin occupied by Lower Dune. In its southern section (Figure 11) slightly down fossil wadi bed, seems to grade laterally into massive floodplain silt.

6—*Middle Dune (Yellow Dune)*—cemented to consolidated dune sand with rare vertical jointings and very inconspicuous and ill-defined lamination, cementation increases toward top, yellow (10YR 8/6) to very pale brown (10YR 8/4). Upper section of dune in basin mottled, showing clear iron enrichment and reduction stains of typical gley character. Sand is silty, light grey (10YR 7/2) to light brownish grey (10YR 6/2), where dune forms a relatively thin bed between two silts (Figure 11). Main body of dune observed along southwestern, outer edge and northeastern edge of basin. On southwestern side, only northeastern slope of dune is preserved (Figures 12, 13 and 15). Upper section of dune contains one or more crust layers, white (10YR 8/1), highly consolidated to highly cemented, showing horizontal root casts when exposed for long time. Crusts are highly calcareous and developed on slopes dipping toward basin (9a); seem to contain Nile silt and are probably associated with beach zone and postdepositional enrichment in CaCO₃. Laterally toward basin, Upper Dune grades into reworked, laminated sands (9b), mottled with gley characteristics, silt pebbles and sandy silt laminae. In center of basin and at margins, these water-reworked sands grade upward into phytogenic small mounds with several Nile silt horizons near their bases (9c), particularly in K–L section (Figure 16). In basin, Upper Dune sands often mottled and show gley characteristics and vertical casts, probably of water reeds. Top truncated.

7—*Floodplain Silt*—along southern and southwestern, outer edge of basin is a massive, dark brown (10YR 4/3) silt, with small blocky structure and well developed slickensides. Top of silt, in areas underlying Upper Dune (or White Dune), is deflationally truncated with several shallow basins. Silt apparently interfingers with Middle Dune and some parts of its lower section may include one or both lower basin silts. A small sandy basin (7a) is observed at top of Floodplain Silt formed in beach zone (Figure 11).

8—*Upper Basin Silt*—brown (10YR 5/3), light yellowish brown (10YR 6/4) to brownish yellow (10YR 6/6) clay, silt and sandy silt forming continuous lens in basin and interfingering with shore dune sands along its northeastern shore (8a). Central section is clayey with coarse blocky structure and deep desiccation cracks (Figure 11) with overlying sands worked into cracks and their walls, suggesting expansion of clays also after deposition of overlying sands and deep desiccation zone. Amount of sand in silt increases toward edges of basin. Upper Basin Silt apparently contemporaneous with upper section of Floodplain Silt. Outcrops on surface in southeastern section of complex. Contains Middle Paleolithic archaeology. Top of Upper Basin Silt truncated in places. Silt clearly fills center of basin and small depressions in its margins (Figure 13), and extends southeastwards toward fossil mouth of lateral wadi.

9—*Upper Dune (White Dune)*—white (10YR 8/1) dune sand, inconspicuously laminated, deposited along southwestern, outer edge and northeastern edge of basin. On southwestern side, only northeastern slope of dune is preserved (Figures 12, 13 and 15). Upper section of dune contains one or more crust layers, white (10YR 8/1), highly consolidated to highly cemented, showing horizontal root casts when exposed for long time. Crusts are highly calcareous and developed on slopes dipping toward basin (9a); seem to contain Nile silt and are probably associated with beach zone and postdepositional enrichment in CaCO₃. Laterally toward basin, Upper Dune grades into reworked, laminated sands (9b), mottled with gley characteristics, silt pebbles and sandy silt laminae. In center of basin and at margins, these water-reworked sands grade upward into phytogenic small mounds with several Nile silt horizons near their bases (9c), particularly in K–L section (Figure 16). In basin, Upper Dune sands often mottled and show gley characteristics and vertical casts, probably of water reeds. Top truncated.

10—*Lower Stabilization Zone*—a brownish yellow (10YR 6/6 to 6/8, but bleached when exposed), calcareous crust, showing numerous horizontal root casts (and destruction of lamination in the underlying 10–15 cm), developed over a clear deflational truncation of Upper Dune sands, particularly in basin. This is a stabilization zone of pedogenic character. Contains Middle Paleolithic archaeology in top.

11—*Sand Sheet*—coarse, conspicuously laminated sand, often poorly sorted, yellow (10YR 8/6) to greyish to light grey (10YR 7/2), sometimes underlain by fine loose sand with white (10YR 8/2), carbonaceous flecks (11a); both occur either over conspicuous truncation or Lower Stabilization Zone. Sand along margins of basins is friable to loose, grading laterally toward basin into very pale brown (10YR 7/4), reworked coarse sand with conspicuous lamination and occasional silt pebbles (11b). Reworked coarse sand in basin is separated by three calcareous

crusts, pale brown (10YR 6/3) in color, bleached when exposed, showing horizontal root casts (11cI, 11cII, 11cIII) and possible enrichment in silt. Along southern margin of basin in area of burial and Site E-82-6, coarse sands are mottled, with iron reduction and enrichment stains of gley character and vertical stem casts (11d). Middle Paleolithic archaeology at base. At higher elevation along southeastern edge of basin, where coarse sands are thickest (sometimes >1 m), upper section is characterized by development of platey carbonates within finer laminae of shingle character. Occasional Middle Paleolithic artifacts within platey sands and on surface on deflated top. Deflated top of Sand Sheet is covered by these shingles (11e).

12—*Upper Stabilization Zone*—a carbonaceous crust, with numerous horizontal root casts and trunks, developed over Sand Sheet on southeastern slope of a low ridge along southeastern edge of basin. Crust is conformable to slope, indicating original surface of Sand Sheet ridge.

13—*Lower Kubbaniyan Silt*—lies above several truncated sediments of Lower Series, often with crumbly or small and medium blocky structure, dark grey (10YR 4/1), very dark grey (10YR 3/1) to grey (10YR 5/1), consolidated to cemented, interfingering with lower portions of Kubbaniyan Dune (14).

14—*Lower Kubbaniyan Dune*—conspicuously laminated, white dune sands with silt horizons in leeward foreset slopes, sometimes grading up into topset beds. Dune heavily truncated by modern deflation. Near center of basin, dune sands interbedded with thin silt layers forming a typical beach zone of a Nile bay formed in basin. Cultural layer of Site E-81-3 is in this interbedded zone (14a). Site E-81-4 is within dune in a shallow deflational swale near edge of basin, and possibly precedes that of E-81-3.

15—*Middle Kubbaniyan Silt*—dark greyish brown (10YR 3/2) silt, deposited before dune barrier and deposition of diatomites over Kubbaniyan Dunes.

16—*Late Kubbaniyan Silt*—on outer edge of dune barrier interfingering with Late Kubbaniyan Dune, beyond later lake formation and, therefore, not altered after deposition.

17—*Late Kubbaniyan Dune*—contemporaneous with and later than Middle Kubbaniyan Silt, part of dune barrier.

18—Recent wadi deposits.

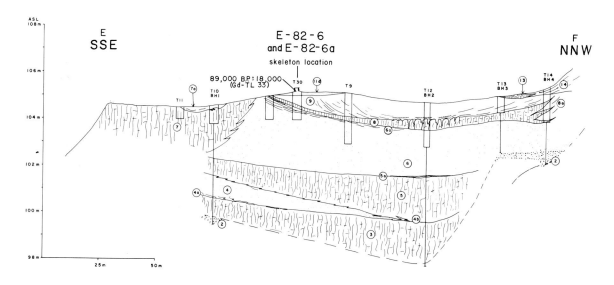

Figure 11. Cross-section E–F. For key, see Figure 10.

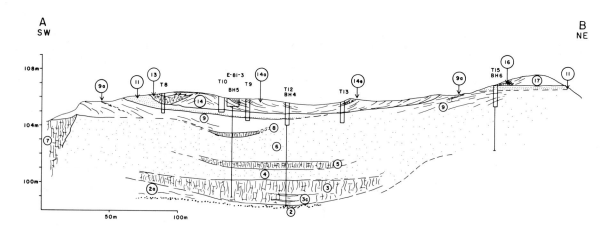

Figure 12. Cross-section A–B. For key, see Figure 10.

Bay and Basin Deposition

The lithostratigraphy and depositional history in the mouth of the small tributary wadi are very complicated, but are also very important for our understanding of the micro-environment of the Middle Paleolithic settlements found in this area.

Nilotic deposition in the bay begins with dark greyish brown to dark brown (10YR 4/2 to 7.5YR 4/2) sandy silt (3), grading into a clayey silt with slickensides and small, columnar-to-blocky structure, which is named the *Lower Basin Silt*. This silt,

particularly its upper portion, shows characteristics of an initial vertisol. Laterally toward the mouth of the bay and perhaps southwestward to the margins of the bay, it formed, by the end of its deposition, part of the main body of floodplain silts (Figures 10 and 11:3a). A shore zone with reworked sand lenses has been observed in places (Figure 10:3b). In the northwestern area of the bay closest to the Nubia Sandstone cliff, several horizons of inblown, yellow dune sand (3c) occur within the bed (Figure 12) and the top of the silt is more sandy.

The deposition of the Lower Basin Silt closely followed the pre-existing morphology. Its maximal

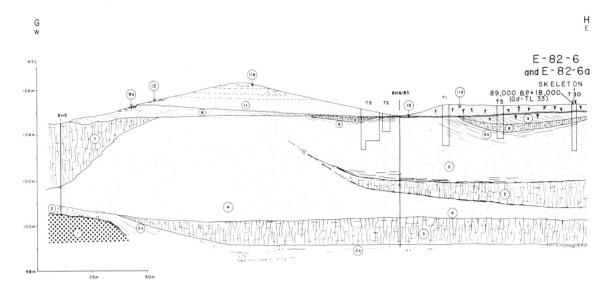

Figure 13. Cross-section G–H. For key, see Figure 10.

thickness is slightly less than 2 m in the center of the bay, near its mouth (Figure 11). The lowest elevation recorded is *ca.* 98 m asl or 8 m above the modern floodplain. The highest elevation recorded is slightly below 101 m asl. The Lower Basin Silt is known only from bore holes; thus its micro-stratigraphic relationship to the massive floodplain clayey sites outside the bay is unknown. It is most likely that in the areas beyond the bay, it forms the lower portion of the apparently homogeneous clays.

The lowest silt is covered by the *Lower Dune* (4), a rather thick bed of light yellowish brown (10YR 6/4) sand which is usually highly cemented and grades into consolidated, very pale brown (10YR 7/4), aeolian sand. The dune is fine-grained and relatively well sorted. Its base is friable and coarse, and seems to represent a thin sand-sheet with original desert coloring (4a). The dune attains its maximal thickness of *ca.* 3 m along the southwestern edge of the bay and slopes down toward its center (Figures 12 and 13:4). Here, where the dune is at its lowest elevation, the sand is light yellowish brown (10YR 6/4) and friable and contains dark brown (7.5YR 4/2) silt lenses (4b), indicating its contemporaneity with the beginning of the deposition of the succeeding basin silt.

The Lower Dune also is known only from bore holes, and could not, therefore, be distinguished from the Middle Dune is those areas where the two are not separated by the Middle Basin Silt (along the

southwestern and northeastern banks of the bay). Its relationship there with the floodplain silt and clays is also inferred from bore holes (Figure 14). It is thought that both the Lower and Middle Dunes interfinger with the floodplain silt and are contemporaneous with the earlier part of it; the later and higher sections of the silt overlie them. The highest elevation of the Lower Dune (extrapolated from the recognised slope) is *ca.* 103 m asl while its base lies slightly below 100 m asl.

The Lower Dune is covered by the *Middle Basin Silt* (5), the earliest bed to be visible in the small deflational windows near the southeastern edge of the bay. It is a highly cemented, pale brown (10YR 6/3), calcareous silt with a 10-cm thick, calcareous crust developed in its topmost part in the middle of the basin (5a). In the center of the basin, the silt reaches its maximal thickness of 2 m and is dark brown (7.5YR 4/2) with small blocky structure. It tapers toward the margins of the bay, except at the mouth where it seems to merge with the main body of the floodplain clayey silts. Its maximal elevation is between 102 and 103 m asl.

The thick *Middle Dune* then filled the basin (6). It is made up of a fine sand, slightly coarser than that of the Lower Dune. It is cemented to consolidated, with rare vertical jointings and inconspicuous lamination masked by carbonate cementation. Its main body lies southwest of the center of the bay, where it immediately covers the earlier dune. Here, it reaches

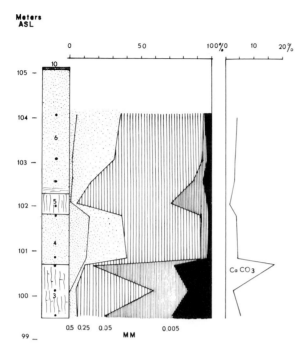

Figure 14. Grain size and calcium carbonate content of sediments from bore hole 8/83 near skeleton on G–H cross-section (Figure 13). For key to units, see Figure 10.

an inferred thickness of slightly less than 3 m and an elevation of *ca*. 105 m asl at its highest point. The dune is exposed on the surface near the mouth of the bay, where it was also probably thick and reached the same elevation as along its southwestern margin. It obviously closed the bay, forming a basin. It is also visible in the small deflational windows near the Middle Paleolithic site of E-82-5. The Middle Dune is yellow (10YR 8/6) to very pale brown (10YR 8/4). In the basin it is mottled with large enrichment and reduction stains. Along the shores of the basin, the yellow dune sand grades near its top into a typical beach zone of rhythmic and semi-rhythmic sand horizons sandwiched between sandy silts (6a). These mark a zone of active beach sedimentation during seasonal flooding and silt deposition. Beyond the basin and along its southwestern margin, the Middle Dune is believed to interfinger with the upper sections of the preserved floodplain clayey silts (7).

In the southeastern area, where it is exposed on the surface, the Middle Dune apparently has a pronounced calcareous crust at the top, developed in a thin, sandy silt layer. The crust occurs on low erosional remnants and overlies a thin (<30 cm) bed of coarse sand-sheet. There are many horizontal root-casts in the crust and the basal parts of several tree trunks, some 30 cm in diameter, were also observed. The exact chrono-stratigraphic position of the crust is not clear. It is most likely, however, that both the crust and the coarse sand-sheet are related to the later episode of sand-sheet deposition (Figure 15:11 and 12), which followed the deflation of the Upper Dune.

The sands and silts of the beach zone grade up into the *Upper Basin Silt* (8), a relatively thin (slightly over 50 cm thick), clayey silt bed, which is brown (10YR 5/3), light yellowish brown (10YR 6/4) to brownish yellow (10YR 6/6) in color. The bed forms a continuous lens in the central part of the basin and tapers toward the northwestern, southern, southwestern and southeastern edges; it interfingers with a descending dune along the northeastern margin (8a). In the center of the basin, the silt is very clayey and shows columnar to coarse blocky structure and deep desiccation cracks cutting through the bed (Figure 11). The overlying sands fill the cracks and are partially worked into their clay walls suggesting syngenetic filling and an active seasonal desiccation zone. Here, the Upper Basin Silt is probably contemporaneous with the uppermost preserved parts of the floodplain clayey silts. A large part of the bed outcrops in the southeastern portion of the area, where it contains isolated quartz flakes and cores, probably of Middle Paleolithic age. The highest elevation of the Upper Basin Silt is *ca*. 105 m asl, along the margins of the basin.

The Upper Basin Silt and the floodplain silts in the southwestern margin of the area (Figures 12, 13 and 15) are immediately overlain by white (10YR 8/1) dune sands (9), which also cover the preceding dunes along the northeastern edge of the basin (Figure 12). These sands form part of an extensive phytogenic dune field. They are fine, well sorted, inconspicuously to conspicuously laminated and conform to the individual shapes of small phytogenic hillocks (Figures 15 and 16). The upper parts of the dunes contain a much higher proportion of fine sands and are better sorted. Truncated and cemented parts of this *Upper Dune* field have been differentially exposed by deflation and may be seen as low rises in the northwestern section of the area (near line A–B of the composite cross-section). The upper parts of the dunes often contain several crusts,

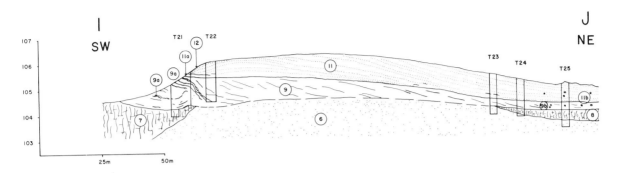

Figure 15. Cross-section I–J. For key, see Figure 10.

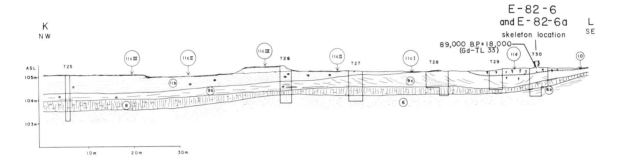

Figure 16. Cross-section K–L. For key, see Figure 10.

which are white (10YR 8/1) and made up of calcium carbonate-cemented sandy silts (9a). These are usually developed on slopes dipping toward the basin (Figure 15) and are clearly deposited over silt horizons left by Nile waters during the peak of the flood (Figure 17).

In the central part of the basin (Figure 16), the sands have been mottled by reduction processes and show gley characteristics, as well as vertical carbonaceous casts—most probably of water-reeds. They were partially reworked by seasonal Nile floods during the early stages of their deposition and contain brownish silt laminae and silt pebbles, indicating seasonal flooding of the basin (9b). Around the center of the basin, the reworked sands grade into small, phytogenic mounds, of which the basal parts include a number of thin, sandy, Nile silt horizons (Figure 16:9c).

The thickness of the white dune sands has been much reduced by later aeolian truncation. However, in the remaining portion, the dune reaches a thickness of almost 1.5 m, and elevations of slightly over

105 m asl in the southwestern portion of the basin and almost 107 m asl near the cliff.

After the deposition of the phytogenic dunes of the upper series, a clear deflational truncation cut through the Upper Dune and into the more elevated portions of the older sediments. This truncation is also marked by the development of a calcareous crust made up of poorly sorted, rather coarse sands cemented by calcium carbonate (10), with a maximal thickness of *ca.* 5 cm. There is a rich network of horizontal root-casts, often of tree size, in the crust. The underlying, 10–15 cm thick zone is brownish yellow (10YR 6/6 to 6/8), and bleaches quickly when exposed. This is the *Lower Stabilization Zone*, which developed after a pronounced truncation, following a lowering of the seasonal peaks of the Nile floods. The surface of the truncation is usually close to 105 m asl in the southwestern section of the area and slightly below 107 m asl near the cliff.

Several small (1–5+ m in diameter), Mousteroid artifact concentrations were found on the surface of

Figure 17. View of calcium carbonate crusts exposed on the eroded surface of the Middle Paleolithic Upper Dune. Deflated artifacts from the Khormusan-related Site E-82-4 occurred just behind the figure.

the Lower Stabilization Zone and in the very base of the overlying sands (11). The quartz artifacts are slightly aeolized, although not rolled. One of the concentrations, Site E-82-5, was collected and partially excavated in the 1982 and 1984 seasons. A few artifacts were also excavated from the same bed near Site E-82-6 in the 1984 season. These small concentrations seem to have been left during a period when the Nile was at a considerably lower level than that of the stabilized zone. The floods probably could not reach the sites, but some marginal vegetation must have been present. The sites may have been occupied seasonally, during the peaks of the floods.

An aeolian *Sand Sheet* developed around the basin above the stabilization surface. This is a relatively thick bed of poorly sorted, horizontally laminated, coarse sand (11), which is yellow (10YR 8/6) or greyish to light grey (10YR 7/2), and is sometimes underlain by fine, loose, white (10YR 8/2) sand with carbonaceous flecks (11a). The Sand Sheet is friable, grading laterally (toward the center of the basin) into a very pale brown (10YR 7/4), reworked, coarse sand with conspicuous lamination and occasional silt pebbles (11b); this sediment has been redeposited by water. Three calcareous crusts (Figure 16:11cI–11cIII) developed in the more silty horizons within the bed. They are pale brown (10YR 6/3), soon bleach when exposed and include numerous horizontal, carbonaceous root-casts.

Along the southern margin of the basin (Figure 16:11d), the Sand Sheet is mottled with gley enrichment and reduction stains, and includes many vertical root-casts (presumably reeds). It was in this area that the early Late Paleolithic grave-pit (Site E-82-6) was cut into the sediment and was preserved because of carbonaceous cementation. A sample of sand from just below the pit and 20 cm above the base of the Sand Sheet gave a thermoluminescence date of 89,000 B.P. ± 18,000 years. (Gd-TL33).

The redeposited coarse sands in the middle of the basin lie at elevations from slightly above 104 m to just over 105 m asl. At higher elevations, along the southwestern margin of the basin in the areas where the Sand Sheet attains its greatest thickness of almost 1.3 m and reaches over 106 m asl, its upper section is characterized by the development of thin platey carbonate crusts within the finer horizons which rhythmically separate the coarse-grained laminae (11e). Today, the thin crust plates litter the deflated bed and resemble shingle. There are occasional quartz artifacts, probably Middle Paleolithic, within the Sand Sheet in this area. Along the northeastern margin of the basin, the sand sheet reaches an elevation of slightly over 107 m asl and further north, closer to the cliff, of *ca.* 109 m asl.

A carbonaceous crust, 10–15 cm thick, developed over the deflated surface of the Sand Sheet (12) and is called the *Upper Stabilization Zone.* It could be seen along the southwestern slope of a low sandy, deflational ridge cut into the Sand Sheet, where the many horizontal root-casts in the crust follow the deflational slope of the ridge (Figure 13). Although the crust is associated with the surface of the Sand Sheet, its age is unknown, but, since it follows a deflational surface and precedes the earliest sediments of the Late Paleolithic episode of Nile Valley filling in this area, it is probable that it developed during this episode of siltation.

In the basin area, the coarse sands are the uppermost preserved sediments of the Middle Paleolithic Nilotic and aeolian sequence. The succeeding sediments are associated with Late Paleolithic occupations and are clearly separated from the underlying Middle Paleolithic deposits by a major deflational unconformity. However, the *Floodplain Silts* continued to accumulate in the Southern Section of the wadi, to an elevation of at least 110.7 m asl at the western edge of the village of Kubbaniya; that is, to a level at least 4 m higher than the uppermost preserved sediments of the Sand Sheet.

Several patches of massive Floodplain Silts of a vertisol-related character are preserved along the southwestern margin of the basin. The silts have been eroded by the recent wadi and are obviously deflated (7); the preserved remnants have been lowered to the level preceding the formation of the Upper Dune (Figures 10, 12 and 13). These silts are clayey, cemented and dark brown (10YR 4/3), with

small-to-medium blocky structure, and have well developed slickensides and rounded calcium carbonate nodules. They seem to interfinger with the Middle Dune and, near the base, with the Lower Dune. A small, sandy, floodplain basin (7a) was observed in the lowered surface of the silts (Figure 11). The minimal recorded thickness of the silts varies from 2 to 3 m (Figures 10 and 11), but the lack of bore-holes away from the basin and the destruction of the silts by the Holocene wadi channel mean that their real thickness cannot be determined. The lowest recorded elevation is at *ca.* 101 m and the highest is at 105 m asl. There is little doubt that the Floodplain Silts adjacent to the basin are a part of the larger floodplain sedimentation which extends across the wadi and is evident in the Southern Section.

Within the same general area of the Northern Section, a thin, but extensive, scatter of Khormusan-related artifacts (Site E-82-4) was found in a lag position on the surfaces of the Sand Sheet, of the Upper Dune and of the Floodplain Silts.

Floodplain and Near-Channel Deposits

At the southeastern tip of the eastern part of the Northern Section is a peninsula of fine, brown, fluviatile sands interbedded with thin horizons of silt. This outcrop is at the foot of a remnant isolated by recent wadis and lies between 102 and 104 m asl. The sands must be contemporaneous with one of the lower basin silts, but their precise stratigraphic relationship is not clear.

On the other side of the recent wadi channel, in the Southern Section (Figure 18), similar sands also outcrop along the footslopes of the Late Quaternary remnant dissected by the modern wadi channel (Figure 19). Here, they underlie and interfinger with the floodplain silts near Site E-78-9. The sands are loose to slightly consolidated, fine to very fine, lustrous, grey to grey-brown in color and contain flecks of mica and numerous heavy minerals. They are laminated to flakey, and dip toward the Nile and toward the center of the wadi. Rare, thin (10–15 cm thick) lenses of sandy brown silt occur within the bed, as well as occasional rounded nodules of calcium carbonate and carbonaceous root-casts (Figure 23). To the west (upstream in Wadi Kubbaniya), these fluvial sands seem to thin out and merge with the massive body of floodplain silt and clays

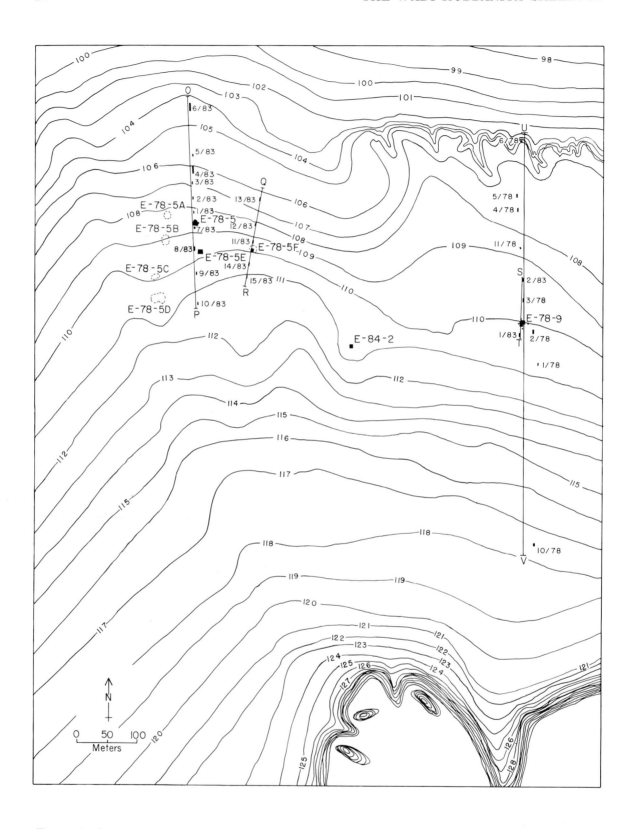

Figure 18. Contour map of south bank area near the mouth of Wadi Kubbaniya. Map prepared by Ali Mazhar.

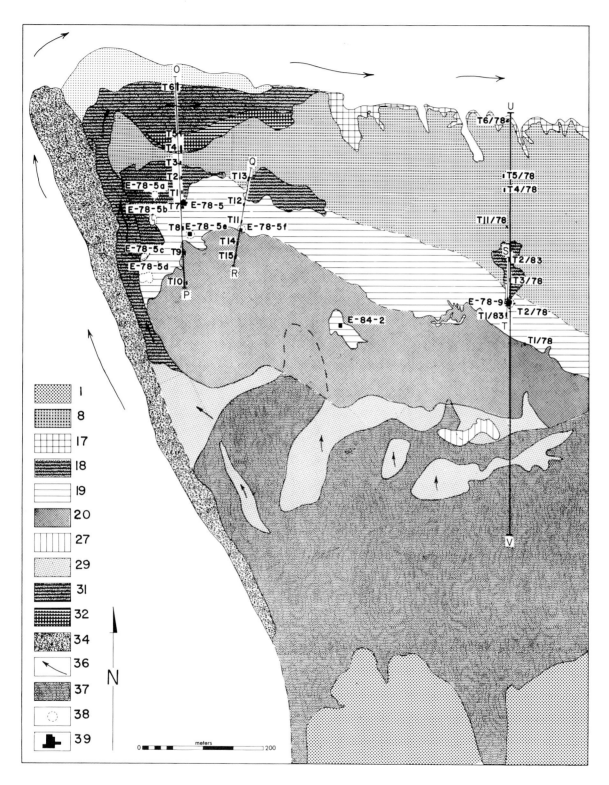

Figure 19. Geological map of south bank area near the mouth of Wadi Kubbaniya. For key to 1–20, 29, 36, 38 and 39, see Figure 8; 27–Upper Kubbaniyan Silt; 31–wadi sands and gravel; 32–wadi silts; 34–wadi gravel; 37–modern sand sheet. Map prepared by Romuald Schild and Ali Mazhar.

which is exposed on the surface near Site E-78-5 (Figure 20). The maximum thickness of the fluvial sands (the base was not exposed) at the bank of the Southern Section, north of Site E-78-9, is about 6.5 m. Their elevation thus ranges from at least 99.5 m to 106 m asl.

A thick bed of Middle Paleolithic floodplain silts outcrops on the surface slightly north of Site E-78-5 and extends unbroken along the bank of the pseudo-terrace cut by the recent wadi east of the village of Kubbaniya. Here, it reaches its highest elevation of 110.7 m asl. Near Site E-78-5, these floodplain silts and clays overlie wadi sands and gravel (Figure 20:1), or fine, light grey (2.5Y 7/2) to light brownish grey (2.5Y 6/2), consolidated, aeolian sands. The seemingly homogeneous bed of clay and silts is made up of clays at the base, which grade into clayey silts in the upper sections. The basal parts have a high index of clay particles (almost 40%) and can be classified within the vertisols, while the upper parts are vertisol-related; the differences probably reflect the ratio of silt deposition and the length of exposure to churning processes.

The clays and clayey floodplain silts (Figure 20:3) are characterized by large-to-medium blocky and columnar structure and well developed slicken-sides. A network of large and deep, polygonal desiccation cracks developed in the upper portion, immediately below the overlying sands. The cracks are filled with brown silty sand and sometimes with the overlying dune sands, (in the latter case, proba-bly in renewed polygons). Lithologically, the clays and clayey silts are homogeneous with no trace of intrusions from other sediments. They are greyish brown (10YR 5/2) to brown (10YR 4/3) and contain numerous secondary calcareous nodules like those found in the eastern part of the Northern Section, across the modern wadi. They reach a maximal thickness of over 5.5 m and lie between *ca.* 101 and 107 m asl near Site E-78-5. They rise toward Site E-78-9, where their top is at nearly 109 m asl, and toward the western margin of the village, where an elevation of 110.7 m has been recorded.

Farther up the wadi, in the western portion of the Northern Section, is a very dark, greyish brown (10YR 3/2), clayey silt, with slickensides and small carbonaceous nodules. It occurs just above the wadi gravel and below the Late Paleolithic dunes and silts near Sites E-78-4, E-78-7 and E-78-8. These dark silts have been reached only in bore holes, but their physical appearance and their clear separation from

the overlying Late Paleolithic silts suggest an asso-ciation with the Middle Paleolithic complex. The silts are relatively thin (*ca.* 1 m thick) and lie between *ca.* 100 and 101 m asl. Their top has probably been lowered by a pronounced deflation. Farther to the north, near Site E-81-7 and Pit A/4, they are not present at all and the Late Paleolithic dune immediately overlies the wadi sands and gravels, at an elevation close to 103 m asl. The older silts here either may have been removed by later deflation or were never deposited because of an intervening dune field.

A truncated bed of aeolian sands (Figure 20 and 21) fills what appear to be deflational basins exca-vated in the top of the Middle Paleolithic floodplain silts and clays at Sites E-78-5 and E-78-9. The bed now consists of the foreset horizons of dunes which were moving toward the south and which have been spared subsequent removal by their deposition in the basins. The dunes are made up of well-sorted, medium and fine-grained sand, which is very pale brown (10YR 8/3) and friable to consolidated (Figures 20 and 22:4). The bedding is completely masked near the top and is inconspicuous in the middle and lower sections. No silts interfinger or interbed with these dune sands, except at the very top where they are reworked.

The dune seems to postdate the highest Middle Paleolithic siltation. The remaining truncated dunes most probably represent a large dune field which developed over the floodplain after it had become inaccessible to the Nile floods. A thermolumines-cence date for the base of the foreset beds in Trench 1 at Site E-78-5 gave an age of 31,000 B.P. ± 8000 years (Gd-TL32). An extremely pronounced defla-tion removed the topset beds and most of the foreset beds of the dune field, except for those sands deposited in the basins. These basin sands were lowered to a level similar to that of the surrounding floodplain silts, and the highest remaining section of the dune field is at an elevation of 109.5 m asl.

The top of the remaining dune sands was re-worked during the subsequent, Late Paleolithic phase of Nile Valley filling, and the remaining patches of dune sand, surrounded by older silts, were an attractive place for human settlement. Two such areas contain extensive debris of human occu-pation: Sites E-78-5 and E-78-9, both of Kubbani-yan affiliation. The topmost 10–20 cm of the sands (Figures 22 and 23:4a) contain rich archaeological materials and fauna, including some *Bulinus* shells.

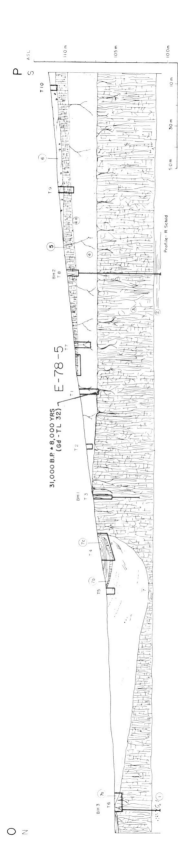

Figure 20. Cross-section O–P.

Key

1–Wadi sands and gravels, base unexposed.

2–fine aeolian (?) sand, light grey (2.5Y 7/2) to light brownish grey (2.5Y 6/2), dull grains, consolidated, base unexposed.

3–massive Middle Paleolithic floodplain silt—vertisol—with medium to large blocky structure, slickensides (large), cemented, CaCO₃ flecks in cracks; top with pronounced desiccation cracks filled with brown silty sand, sometimes with Unit 4 (renewed polygons); greyish brown (10YR 5/2) to brown (10YR 4/3), numerous small calcareous pebbles.

4–Post-Middle Paleolithic Dune, topset beds, truncated at top with slight dip toward south, clearly laminated, medium to coarse grained, friable to cemented at top, very pale brown (10YR 8/3); 4a–same dune top section with

bedding destroyed by soil, large blocky structure, cemented, heavy concentration of CaCO₃, possible pedogenic alterations of top, coarse grains (dull), white (10YR 8/1); Kubbaniyan artifacts and rare *Bulinus* shells worked in at top; truncated both before human occupation and recently, traces of burrowing animals with overlying silt fillings.

5–Lower Kubbaniyan Silt, cemented with medium to small blocky structure and slickensides, vertisol, dark grey (15YR 4/1); contains occasional traces of archaeology in Tr. 11 of Site E-78-5f; deep desiccation cracks; grey in areas waterlogged below dune (Unit 6).

6–Lower Kubbaniyan Dune (later part) probably combining also Upper Kubbaniyan Dune in higher sections; foreset beds with *Bulinus* shells and silt streaks on

leeward sides of dune, friable, recently truncated; carbonaceous roots similar to those in main Lower Kubbaniyan Dune; contains Ballanan assemblage at base (E-78-5f); friable, conspicuously laminated; upper, unexposed sections probably contemporaneous with Upper Kubbaniyan Dune and forming part of dune barrier.

7–Early Holocene wadi channel; lower portion (7a) of friable, conspicuously laminated sands and gravel with large pebbles of redeposited diatomite and Kubbaniyan silt; upper channel filled with brownish silts with medium blocky structure, cemented (7b) probably redeposited Kubbaniyan silt; above (7c) conspicuously laminated fine sands or gravels of reworked, cemented older silts and fine sands; silty fill probably deposited on playa in closed (blocked) wadi.

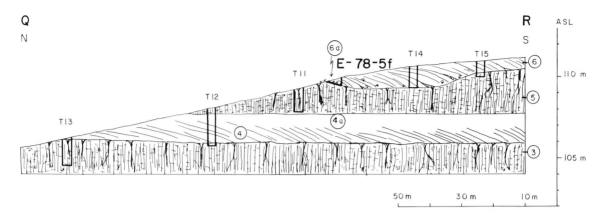

Figure 21. Cross-section Q–R. For key, see Figure 20.

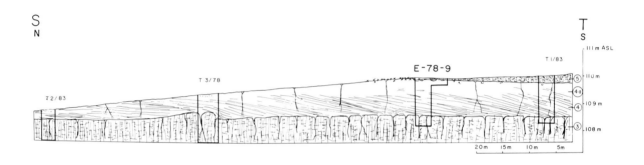

Figure 22. Cross-section S–T. For key, see Figure 20.

The lithic artifacts have a typical, fine particle polish. The reworked sand is very pale brown (10YR 7/3) and contains thin, horizontal streaks of silt. It is usually highly cemented and carbonaceous, with small vertical jointing. A radiocarbon date of 18,230 B.P. ± 200 years (SMU-1226) has been obtained on *Unio* shells from the cultural layer at Site E-78-9. Both the date and the archaeological content of the reworked zone indicate association of the reworking with an early part of the Late Paleolithic raising of the Nile floodplain.

Heavy Minerals

Information concerning the major heavy mineral components of the modern Nile and its tributaries comes from the work of Shukri (1950, 1951) and Shukri and Azer (1952), who tested modern sediments from the main tributaries of the Nile. There is only limited knowledge of the heavy mineral suites

of Late Pleistocene and Recent Nilotic sediments, but the results of heavy mineral analyses of the sediments associated with the Middle Paleolithic valley-filling are, nevertheless, of interest.

It is generally believed that four heavy mineral groups—the opaques, amphiboles, pyroxenes and epidotes—form the most characteristic and diagnostic complex. Their frequencies in the two major systems of Nile tributaries, the Ethiopian and the White Nile systems, seem to differ significantly: the opaque minerals and epidotes are more frequent in the White Nile system; the pyroxenes are extremely rare in the White Nile system but rather frequent in the Blue Nile and Atbara; and the amphiboles are very frequent in the Blue Nile, rare in the Atbara and quite frequent in the White Nile.

The Middle Paleolithic Nilotic silts in Wadi Kubbaniya are characterized by a rather high frequency of the opaques (*ca.* 33%), followed by amphiboles (*ca.* 33%, composed of hornblende,

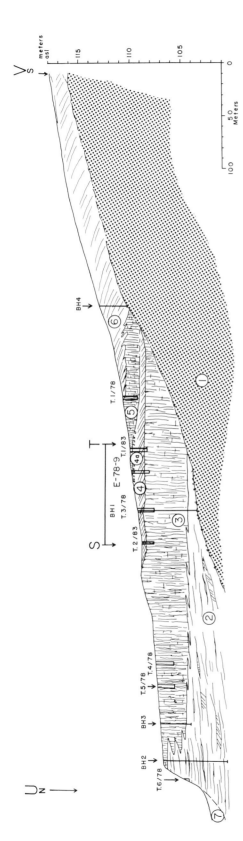

Figure 23. Cross-section U–V.

Key

1—Nubia sandstone.

2—loose to consolidated, fine to very fine, fluvial sands with mica and heavy minerals, laminated or flakey, dipping towards the Nile and the center of the wadi; contains small, rare, CaCO₃ concretions and rare, thin (10–15 cm) layers and lenses of medium, angular, blocky, brown silt; grey to grey brown.

3—massive Middle Paleolithic floodplain silt—vertisol—with medium to low large blocky structure, slickensides (large), cemented, CaCO₃ flecks in cracks; top with pronounced desiccation cracks filled with brown silty sand, sometimes with Unit 4 (renewed polygons); greyish brown (10YR 5/2) to brown (10YR 4/3) numerous small calcareous pebbles.

4—Post-Middle Paleolithic Dune, topset beds, truncated at top with slight dip toward south, clearly laminated, medium to coarse grained, friable to cemented at top, very pale brown (10YR 8/3); 4a–same dune top section with bedding destroyed by soil, large blocky structure, cemented, heavy concentration of CaCO₃, possible pedogenic alterations of top, coarse grains (dull), white (10YR 8/1); Kubbaniyan artifacts and rare *Bulinus* shells worked in at top; truncated both before human occupation and recently, traces of burrowing animals with overlying silt fillings.

5—Lower Kubbaniyan Silt, cemented with medium to small blocky structure and slickensides, vertisol, dark

grey (15YR 4/1); contains occasional traces of archaeology in Tr. 11 of Site E-78-5f; deep desiccation cracks; grey in areas waterlogged below dune (Unit 6).

6—Lower Kubbaniyan Dune (later part) probably combining also Upper Kubbaniyan Dune in higher sections; foreset beds with *Bulinus* shells and silt streaks on leeward sides of dune, friable, recently truncated; carbonaceous roots similar to those in main Lower Kubbaniyan Dune; contains Ballanan at base (E-78-5f); friable, conspicuously laminated; upper, unexposed sections probably contemporaneous with Upper Kubbaniyan Dune and forming part of dune barrier.

7—modern aeolian sand.

mostly green) and epidotes (*ca.* 20%). Pyroxenes are extremely rare (<3%). Comparison with the heavy mineral suite from the Late Paleolithic Nilotic sediments in Wadi Kubbaniya shows a general similarity of indices, except for the pyroxenes which are more than twice as frequent in the later deposits. Comparison between the heavy minerals from the Middle Paleolithic basin and floodplain silts, however, shows a very high enrichment in chlorite in the vertisols and vertisol-related floodplain beds, reaching a maximum of nearly 36% of the total. This high frequency of chlorite seems to result from the *in situ* metamorphosis of biotite, probably because of the very acidic environment in the vertisols. The low frequencies of biotite in the basin silts are due to its removal in suspension during the processing of the samples. Except for the chlorites, all of the heavy minerals recovered from samples collected in the Nilotic sediments show very heavy transport abrasion. In general, heavy mineral suites from Middle Paleolithic deposits in Wadi Kubbaniya resemble that of the modern Nile, except for the significant differences in the frequencies of pyroxenes and epidotes. Today, the former are much higher while the latter are lower.

There are considerable differences between the results published by Butzer and Hansen for Kom Ombo (1968) and those from Wadi Kubbaniya. Although the Kom Ombo series are derived from three formations, they are generally similar to each other. They differ from the Wadi Kubbaniya Middle Paleolithic series principally in their lower frequencies of opaques, amphiboles and epidotes, and higher indices of pyroxenes. Some of the differences result simply from statistical treatments, since those from Kom Ombo include altered and unidentifiable grains. Comparison with the samples published by Hassan (1976a, 1976b) also shows much lower frequencies of pyroxenes and higher frequencies of epidotes in the Kubbaniya suite.

Full explanation of these differences in results is beyond the scope of this publication; however, they are only partially due to the varying statistical treatments of the samples. The results obtained in Wadi Kubbaniya suggest that the contributions to the main Nile of the Atbara and the Blue Nile, during the late Middle Paleolithic, were much reduced and that most of the water, although still not necessarily a great amount of water, was coming from the White Nile basin. As today, the discharge of the White Nile was probably quite consistent

throughout the year. These conclusions differ from those of Butzer and Hansen, but it is possible that the sediments which they analysed were not of Middle Paleolithic age.

Chronology and River Behavior

The Middle Paleolithic Nilotic sequence postdates the last Late Pleistocene episode of local rainfall and resultant wadi activity. According to data obtained at Bir Sahara and Bir Tarfawi (Wendorf and Schild 1980), this period was associated with an early Aterian. It is, therefore, probable that the entire Middle Paleolithic sequence of Wadi Kubbaniya falls within the hyper-arid period which separates the Aterian and Holocene wet events in the Eastern Sahara. However, the sequence does not represent the entire period of hyper-aridity, since the later part of this period also included the Late Paleolithic phase of Nile Valley filling, which is dated at Wadi Kubbaniya beteen at least 21,000 and 12,000 B.P.

It is likely that the Nile sediments associated with the Middle Paleolithic Site 440 in the Khor Musa and with the Khormusan industry at Wadi Halfa, northern Sudan, should be included in the period of Middle Paleolithic valley-filling recorded in Wadi Kubbaniya. The Khormusan sites in Sudanese Nubia vary considerably in relative elevation, between 11 m and 28 m above the modern floodplain, and it is believed that the group of lower sites (6G27, 6G30 and ANW-3) were associated with an early phase of downcutting which followed the maximum rise of the floodplain. The highest Khormusan sites probably date to a late phase of the Middle Paleolithic valley-filling and are certainly older than 41,500 B.P. (Wendorf *et al.* 1979). The thermoluminescence date, from the foreset beds of the dune which postdates the highest Middle Paleolithic siltation in Wadi Kubbaniya, accords with this hypothesis. The high marls in Wadi Or in Nubia, believed to date to the Korosko Formation of Butzer and Hansen (1968:96), may mark the end of the same accumulation. Their date of 27,200 B.P. +1000/−900 (I-2061) was near the top of the local sequence and, since it was measured on carbonates, indicates the minimal age of the sample.

The Middle Paleolithic Nile accumulation in Wadi Kubbaniya was not a uniform and monotonous episode of constant sediment building and raising of the river bed, despite the apparent homogeneity of the floodplain clays and silts, particularly in the Southern Section. The sequence in the basin clearly indicates at least one period of lower water, as seen in the truncation of the Upper Dune. The accumulation of a sand sheet above the truncation suggests a period of relative stability, during which the basin was flooded at the peak flood but the water soon receded, leaving the basin open to aeolian activity. It is not clear when the carbonaceous crusts developed in these sediments; it is possible that all of them postdate the Middle Paleolithic sequence and are more or less contemporaneous with the accumulation of the carbonates in the Late Paleolithic grave-pit.

During the Middle Paleolithic sequence in Wadi Kubbaniya, sediments aggraded from at least 98 m asl to 110.5 m asl, or from 8 m to 20.5 m above the modern floodplain. Throughout, the Nilotic sediment accumulation is associated with intensive aeolian deposition along the northern cliff, as a result of the entrapment of sand by vegetation. The overall pattern of simultaneous silt and dune accumulation is the same as that of the Late Paleolithic phase of valley filling. These similarities suggest that both the Middle Paleolithic and Late Paleolithic phases of Nile Valley filling were the results of analogous climatic phenomena. It is known that the Late Paleolithic Nilotic accumulation was coeval with hyper-aridity in the Sahara, low water discharge of both the Blue and the White Niles and low lake stands across the central African belt. The main Nile was therefore receiving much less water from these two systems and the discharge was highly seasonal. The competence of the Nile must have been reduced while its capacity and sediment load may have been greatly increased. This incompetence and extreme seasonality led to the accumulation of sediments and to the development of intensively braided, shallow channels, which caused a more or less steady rise in both the channel and the floodplain.

In contrast, the periods of greater water discharge in the catchment areas increased the competence of the Nile and, because of slope stabilization due to denser vegetation in areas of higher rainfall, reduced its sediment load, all of which induced downcutting. The higher discharge in the headwaters did not coincide with local rainfall in southern Egypt, as is shown by the lack of any traces of runoff or slope movement in Wadi Kubbaniya during the downcutting period between the Middle and Late Paleolithic Nilotic complexes.

The histories of the Middle Paleolithic Blue and White Niles are essentially unknown. A lowered discharge before 40,000 B.P. is suggested by a few radiocarbon dates on evaporites, ranging from >40,000 B.P. (SUA-382), to 36,800 B.P. +3,100/ −2,200 years (SUA-381), to 25,600 B.P. ± 700 years (SUA-837). obtained from a desiccated White Nile lake near Esh Shaval in Sudan (Adamson *et al.* 1982:201). This episode may have been coeval with the formation of massive carbonate beds in the Gezira fan, which today are found as allochthonous carbonate nodules in later sediments and have been dated by radiocarbon to >40,000 B.P. (Adamson *et al.* 1982:172).

The chronologies of the lake and river levels for Equatorial and East Africa for the period prior to 20,000 years ago are also controversial. Almost all of the radiocarbon dates are on carbonates, which are highly susceptible to secondary rejuvenation by contamination and leaching of younger carbonates. The archaeological associations have not been studied and thus cannot be used as a more precise means of dating. It is evident that the Final Pleistocene period of aridity was preceded by several intervals of higher lake stands and intervening dry phases (Gasse and Street 1978; Gasse *et al.* 1980). However, the available radiocarbon dates for these lake levels conflict with the chronology of the late Middle Paleolithic valley-filling in the main Nile Valley and the succeeding period of downcutting. The East African climatic events, therefore, cannot be related precisely to the Nile sequence. Instead, it is believed that the late Middle Paleolithic aggradation reflects climatic phenomena closely similar to those of the Late Paleolithic valley-filling. It probably took place during a period of reduced discharge from the main Nile tributaries, and coincided with increased slope erosion and sediment load; the period of downcutting, which began prior to 30,000 years ago, may have been the result of increased flow and reduced aridity in the Nile headwaters. It should be noted that there is no evidence of increased local rainfall at this time in the Eastern Sahara or elsewhere in Egypt and northern Sudan.

Late Paleolithic Valley Filling Episode

A pronounced deflation may have removed as much as 3–4 m of sediment, including clayey floodplain silt, in the basin area and even more in the western portion of Northern Section. There was then a new period of valley-filling. The earliest recorded sediments of this period in Wadi Kubbaniya are at 102 m asl and the latest are at *ca.* 117–118 m asl, or from 12 m to 27–28 m above the modern floodplain. The earliest dates for these sediments are about 20,500 B.P. (Site E-81-4), while the youngest are about 12,500 B.P. (the recessional beach at Site E-81-5). After the aggradation of the floodplain and the formation of a seepage lake behind a dune barrier, a downcutting began which removed at least part of the barrier and led to the deposition of the latest silts above the lacustrine sediments. There are no radiocarbon dates, but this period is estimated to date to *ca.* 12,000 B.P. The first local rains appeared soon afterwards, creating sandy and silty playa basins in the wadi.

A detailed account of the Late Paleolithic period of floodplain accumulation in Wadi Kubbaniya is beyond the scope of this summary, but a few observations are of importance. First of all, the grave-pit at Site E-82-6 must already have been dug by a very early stage of the Late Paleolithic floodplain aggradation. The pit did not contain any sediments other than the sands derived from the Sand Sheet; the surface from which the pit was sunk was, therefore, a deflational one which did not bear younger sediments. Late Paleolithic silts were not present when the burial occurred, but they must have been present over the grave-pit from around 20,500 B.P. until very recently, when they were removed by deflation and wash. In this case, the grave is older than the two settlements of E-81-3 and E-81-4, located nearby and dated to about 20,000 B.P. These two settlements are on the seasonal beach of the reexcavated basin and are embedded in Nilotic sediments intercalating with rewashed aeolian sands. The sediments represent an early phase of the Late Paleolithic accumulation. The data at hand suggest that the grave was dug before the deposition of the first Late Paleolithic Nilotic sediments at this elevation (*ca.* 105.5 m asl), and was located beyond the reach of the peak flood, in what was then low desert. If so, the skeleton should date prior to 20,000 B.P., but, because of its Late Paleolithic archaeological associations, no earlier than the beginning of the Late Paleolithic.

A uranium/thorium date of 6500 B.P. $\pm$ 1000 years was obtained on the carbonate matrix which encrusted the skeleton (by B. Szabo of the Branch Isotope Geology Laboratory of the U.S. Geological Survey). The lithostratigraphic, archaeological and anatomical data conflict with such a late age and reflect the vulnerability of the method. It is believed that the development of the calcium carbonate crust in the pit was generally coeval with the formation of the carbonaceous vegetation casts which are so well represented in the Late Paleolithic dunes nearby, dating from *ca.* 20,000 to 17,500 years B.P.

CHAPTER 3

THE ARCHAEOLOGICAL SITES

by

Fred Wendorf and Romuald Schild

Five archaeological sites were recorded in the vicinity of the burial and clearly belong to two distinct intervals of time. The first group, which includes Sites E-82-5, E-82-6a and E-82-4, is Middle Paleolithic in age, while Sites E-81-3 and E-81-4 are Late Paleolithic. Other (unrecorded) scatters of deflated Late Paleolithic artifacts occurred on the aeolian sand to the east of the skeleton, while isolated, but apparently Middle Paleolithic, pieces were found on and in (a few were *in situ*) the sediments of the earlier complex of sands and silts exposed along the southern edge of the basin.

THE MIDDLE PALEOLITHIC OCCUPATION

Site E-82-5

This concentration of artifacts is located about 25 m southeast of the burial, and was mostly deflated but slightly *in situ* (Figure 24). It is associated with the pedogenic horizon, or surface of stabilization, and lies below the base of the aeolian sand sheet which completes the preserved portion of the first cycle of aggradation in the basin. In the area of the site (Figure 25), the aeolian sand sheet has been almost completely removed by deflation, leaving only a thin veneer, 0–5 cm thick. However, about 150 m to the west the sand sheet is 2 m thick and stands as a low hillock. Since a sample of the lowest part of the sand sheet has been dated by thermoluminescence to about 89,000 B.P., Site E-82-5 must be older than that, although how much older cannot be determined: the surface of stabilization represents an unknown length of time when calcium carbonate was being deposited slightly below the surface through a pedogenic process. The site was probably at or very near the edge of the highest reach of the Nile, on a sandy ridge adjacent to a very shallow basin which was seasonally flooded.

Site E-82-5 yielded nothing but lithic artifacts, and all of them, even those which were still *in situ* and buried below the sand sheet, were somewhat wind-abraded, indicating that they had been on the surface when the sand sheet began to accumulate

over them. The collection includes 1480 pieces of debitage, of which the most numerous are chips of quartz, quartzitic sandstone and basalt (Table 1). There were a few chips of chert, agate and Egyptian flint, but these were all on the surface and are probably the result of admixture from the Late Paleolithic sites nearby. The next most frequent class of debitage is unidentified flakes, again almost entirely of quartz, quartzitic sandstone and basalt. Primary flakes, flakes from single platform cores and flakes from multiple platform cores are also present. A single quartz Levallois preparation flake completes the debitage list.

The collection includes 15 cores (Table 2), of which seven are the globular, unpatterned, multiple platform type for the production of flakes, six are unclassifiable fragments, one is a unifacial sub-discoidal core and the last is an initially struck pebble. Quartz, quartzitic sandstone and basalt were the only raw materials represented. The cores tend to be large, with lengths ranging from 38 to 73 mm, widths of 23–59 mm and thicknesses of 22–59 mm. They are poorly utilized and obviously do not represent the majority of the cores which were exploited at the site and which produced the debitage found there. Many cores must have been taken elsewhere when the site was abandoned.

There are 21 retouched tools and unretouched Levallois flakes from Site E-82-5 (Table 3). The Levallois flakes are both atypical; only one has a measurable platform, which is dihedral and struck at an angle of 92°. Nearly half of the collection are denticulates, mostly made on large quartzitic sandstone flakes but with considerable variety in the placement and character of the retouch. Three have the denticulations near the sinister distal end, on two the denticulations are across the distal end, on two others the denticulations are along the entire dexter edge, and there are single examples each with denticulations along the entire sinister edge, bilateral convergent, and on the mid-section of the dexter edge. On three the denticulations are formed by single blows, on three others they are both single-blow and retouched, and on four they are only

Figure 24. View of Middle Paleolithic Site E-82-5, partially exposed by deflation. Note the scatter of lithic artifacts around figure.

retouched. On four the denticulations are inverse, on four they are obverse and on two they are alternating. The complete denticulates range from 23 to 78 mm in length, from 28 to 68 mm in width and from 7 to 25 mm in thickness.

All of the notches are on fragments of large flakes; they all have obverse single-blow notches along the sinister edge, two near the proximal end and the other near the middle. One is made on a primary flake.

One of the retouched pieces has flat inverse retouch along the center of the dexter edge; on the other there is fine obverse retouch along the sinister edge near the distal end. It is the only complete example and measures 33×33×11 mm.

The two sidescrapers are both on broken quartz flakes, one of them Levallois. Both have obverse retouch along the entire remaining portion of the sinister edge. The convergent sidescraper is asym-

metrical, both retouched edges are convex and there is invasive retouch across the end and along both sides near the distal end. This piece is complete and is made on a primary quartz flake, measuring 55×49×12 mm.

The final tool in the collection is a fragment of a battered quartz cobble, showing considerable use as a hammerstone.

Summary of Site E-82-5

The collection from Site E-82-5 is too poor for detailed characterization. However, the simple tool assemblage, with stress on denticulates and side-scrapers, strongly suggests an assemblage which can be placed within the general Mousteroid complex of the Middle Paleolithic, and specifically the Denticulate Mousterian. The Levallois technique is

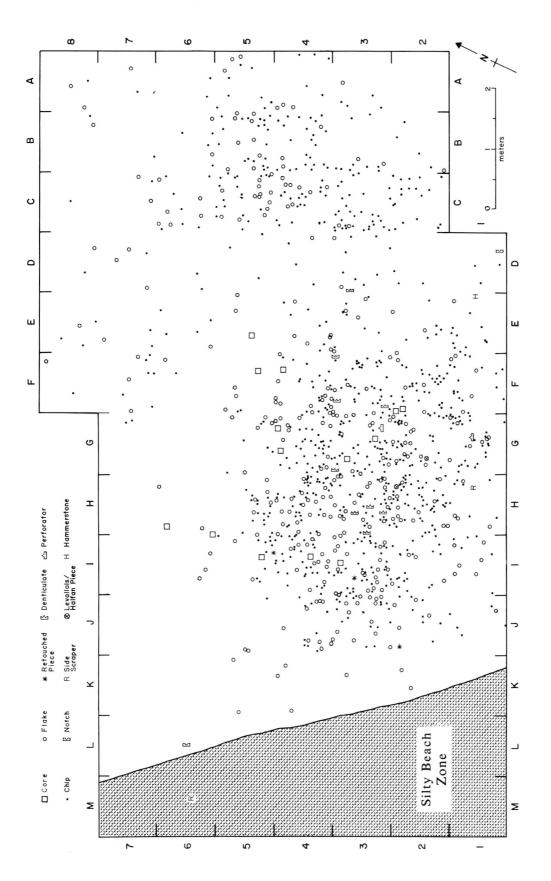

Figure 25. Scatter pattern of lithic artifacts, surface and excavated, from Site E-82-5.

TABLE 1

Debitage Types and Raw Materials from Site E-82-5

Debitage Type	Chert	Agate	Quartz	Quartzitic Sandstone	Flint	Basalt	Ferruginous Sandstone	Total
Primary Flakes			42	15		2		59
Flakes from Single Platform Cores			15	6				21
Flakes from Multiple Platform Cores			24	27		7		58
Unidentified Flakes			91	51		24	1	167
Levallois Preparation Flake			1					1
Chips and Chunks	9	1	888	229	3	43	1	1174
Total	9	1	1061	328	3	76	2	1480

present but was not important: only one retouched tool was made on a Levallois flake, there were only two unretouched Levallois pieces and there were no Levallois cores. This assessment of the lithic assemblage is in close agreement with the age indicated by thermoluminescence of more than 89,000 years ago.

Site E-82-4

Some 125 m southwest of Site E-82-5 is a very dispersed cluster of heavily aeolized lithic artifacts on the eroded surface of the floodplain silts and upper dune, which form the most recent units in the Middle Paleolithic depositional sequence in the wadi. This cluster, about 10 m in diameter, was named Site E-82-4. It is of significance here because the assemblage has some resemblances to the Khormusan, a complex known from several sites near Wadi Halfa in northern Sudan. The Khormusan is regarded as the most recent of the Middle Paleolithic complexes in the Nile Valley, and it has several associated radiocarbon dates of more than 40,000 years old (Wendorf *et al.* 1979).

The collection from Site E-82-4 is not large. It consists of 13 retouched tools, five unretouched Levallois flakes and points, four cores and two burin spalls, making a total of 24 pieces in all. These are listed in Table 4. These were all of the artifacts in the site area except for a few flakes. Debitage was rare, and none of it was collected. It is not certain that this is a valid assemblage of artifacts from a single cultural context, but the absence of other clusters of

artifacts in the vicinity would lend support to this assumption.

The Levallois cores are all for flakes. Two are unstruck, the third is struck. There is considerable range in the preparation of the back. On the struck core the back is not prepared, while the back of one the others is completely prepared, and the third still retains some cortex. All of them have faceted platforms at angles of 80°–85° from the flaking surface. Two of the cores and the core fragment are made of chert, the fourth is of flint.

Among the Levallois flakes and points, three are made on chert and two are on flint. Only two are complete: a typical Levallois flake is 30×19×3 mm, and an atypical Levallois point is 34×25×5 mm.

TABLE 2

Core-Types and Raw Materials from Site E-82-5

Core Type	Quartz	Quartzitic Sandstone	Basalt	Total
Multiple Platform, Unpatterned	4	2	1	7
Subdiscoidal, Unifacial			1	1
Initially Struck		1		1
Fragments	5	1		6
Total	9	4	2	15

TABLE 3

Retouched Tools and Raw Materials from Site E-82-5

Tool-Type	Quartz	Quartzitic Sandstone	Basalt	Granite	Total
Levallois Flakes	1	1			2
Denticulates	3	6	1		10
Notches	2			1	3
Retouched Pieces		1	1		2
Sidescrapers	2				2
Convergent Sidescraper	1				1
Hammerstone	1				1
Total	10	8	2	1	21

The fragments include one distal and two proximal pieces. Three of the platforms are faceted (two are convex, one is straight), and the fourth is *lisse*.

The sidescraper group includes only one simple convex piece. It is made on a broken, primary, quartz flake, and is retouched along the entire remaining portion of the dexter edge. The scraper retouch is 10 mm in height. There are two convergent sidescrapers. One of these is fragmentary and has convex scraping edges. On the sinister edge the scraper retouch is 5 mm high, while the retouch on the dexter edge is rather flat and only 3 mm high. It is made on a tertiary flint flake. The other convergent sidescraper is on a tertiary chert flake, measuring 35×17×9 mm, and has a convex sinister edge with retouch 9 mm high, and a concave dexter edge with scraper retouch 7 mm high. The retouch is strong and occurs along the entirety of both lateral edges. There are two transverse straight sidescrapers, both on chert, one primary (20×29×9 mm) and the other tertiary (broken). Both are slightly *déjeté* and very well made, with scraper retouch 5 mm high.

The collection includes only one endscraper. It is a well made shouldered scraper on an unstruck, quartz, Levallois core which had been competely prepared on both faces; it measures 40×38×11 mm. The shoulder is formed by a large, single-blow notch, and the adjacent scraper retouch is 8 mm high.

One of the burins is a typical, symmetrical, dihedral burin at the distal end of a tertiary flint flake, measuring 26×20×9 mm. One edge had been struck twice, the other only once. The second burin is atypical and made on a chunk of flint, probably a fragment of a core (30×29×10 mm). It is a sym-metrical burin on a truncation, and it was struck only once. The collection also contains two burin spalls, both of flint. Neither could be reconnected to the burins from the site and both are, in fact, considerably longer than the burins. Both are initial spalls without retouch. The largest is 45 mm long, and was probably struck from a Levallois flake. The other, 38 mm long, is overpassed.

The borer is made on a proximal fragment of a tertiary flint piece, probably a blade, with obverse retouch along the entire remaining sinister edge, and

TABLE 4

Cores and Retouched Tools from Site E-82-4

	Bordes Types	Total
	Levallois cores	3
	Fragment of core	1
1	Levallois flake, typical	2
3	Levallois points	3
10	Sidescraper, simple complex	1
19	Sidescraper, convergent convex	1
20	Sidescraper, convergent concavo-convex	1
22	Sidescraper, transverse straight	2
30	Endscraper, typical	1
32	Burins, typical	1
33	Burins, atypical	1
34	Borer, typical	1
40	Truncated piece	1
42	Notched piece	1
43	Denticulate piece	1
62	Retouched flake	1
	Burin spall	2
	Total	24

limited obverse retouch on the central portion of the dexter edge.

The truncated piece is made on a tertiary flint flake, measuring 26×20×3 mm. The truncation is concave, at the distal end, from the dexter edge, and formed by steep obverse retouch. The angle of the truncation is 120° to the axis of the piece. It also has a small shallow obverse retouched notch, 7×1.5 mm, near the distal end of the sinister edge.

The notched piece is made on a broken primary basalt flake, and the notch, 17 mm long and 2 mm deep, is near the center of the dexter edge, and is formed by an obverse single blow. The denticulate is poorly made. It is on a basalt Levallois flake with single blow denticulations at the distal end.

The final piece in the collection is a typical, Levallois, flint flake, with obverse bilateral retouch near the proximal end. It measures 26×20×5 mm.

Summary of Site E-82-4

The only lithic industry known from the Nile Valley which is characterized by a high frequency of Levallois flake technology, many sidescrapers and endscrapers, and numerous burins is the Khormusan, which occurs at several sites near Wadi Halfa in northern Sudan. The assemblage from Site E-82-4 shares these characteristics with the Khormusan, but there are also a number of differences. For example, the Khormusan has much higher frequencies of burins: in some sites they exceed 40% of all retouched tools. Endscrapers (except in what is regarded as the oldest Khormusan assemblage, Site 34A) also tend to be more frequent, usually equaling or exceeding the values for sidescrapers. Finally, borers are not recorded from the Khormusan. Perhaps the most significant of these differences is in the burins, but whether this reflects a functional specialization or some other factor cannot be evaluated, particularly with the limited sample recovered from Site E-82-4.

As a Khormusan-related assemblage, however, Site E-82-4 provides a useful chronological indicator for the early basin silts in Wadi Kubbaniya. The Khormusan sites at Wadi Halfa occur within and on the upper part of the oldest unit of Nile silts recognized in that area. The only other Middle Paleolithic entities in the area which could be tied to this alluvial event are the two Aterian-related occupations at Site 440, which occur in a dune at the base

of these earliest silts. The several Mousterian sites recorded in the area are all on the tops of inselbergs and cannot be tied to the alluvial sequence, but they are believed to predate the earliest silts. The deflated assemblage from Site E-82-4 lay on the surface of the most recent preserved units in the Middle Paleolithic, Nilotic, alluvial sequence in Wadi Kubbaniya. They suggest that other silts, equivalent to the Khormusan-age silts at Wadi Halfa, may once have been present in Wadi Kubbaniya, but were subsequently removed during the interval of erosion and downcutting which preceded accumulation of the Late Paleolithic silts in this area.

Site E-82-6a

The human burial was designated Site E-82-6. After the burial was removed for shipment to Cairo, a trench 4 m long and 1 m wide was dug immediately below where the skeleton had been (Trench 30/82). Several quartz and quartzitic sandstone chips and flakes were found at the base of the sand sheet (Unit 11), and in the top of the underlying white dune (Unit 9). In 1984, in an effort to recover a larger sample and perhaps to identify a living surface, the trench was expanded to 4 m long and 3 m wide. The results, however, were disappointing: only a few additional chips and flakes were recovered and the artifacts seem to represent only limited use of the spot. This is named Site E-82-6a and the recovered debitage is recorded in Table 5.

All of the artifacts are quartz, except for two of the chips, the flake from the multiple platform core

TABLE 5

Debitage and Tools from Site E-82-6a

Type	Number
Primary flakes	4
Flakes from single platform cores	3
Flakes from multiple platform cores	1
Unidentified flakes	6
Chips	32
Total Debitage	46
Levallois flakes, typical	2
Levallois flakes, atypical	1
Denticulate	1
Total	4

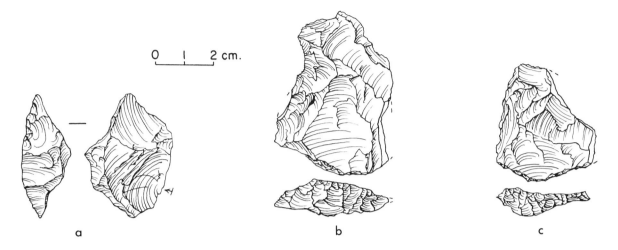

Figure 26. Middle Paleolithic artifacts from Site E-82-6a, at base of Sand Sheet at contact with White Dune. a–Retouched notch; b, c–Levallois flakes.

and the denticulate, which are of similar colored quartzitic sandstone. The denticulate is poorly made. It has two obverse, single-blow denticulations at the distal end, and measures 31×34×16 mm (Figure 26:a).

Miscellaneous Middle Paleolithic Artifacts

Occasional Levallois cores, flakes and other artifacts, made on quartz and quartzitic sandstone, occur scattered on the surface of the uppermost units of the Middle Paleolithic basin fill. Several of these are illustrated in Figure 27. They are typical of the Middle Paleolithic, and are of interest primarily as another indication that these upper units of basin fill were succeeded by more recent Middle Paleolithic occupations. In this instance, the artifacts do not form concentrations, but occur as a thin scatter over an area about 50 m in diameter, some 30 m northwest of the burial pit.

THE LATE PALEOLITHIC OCCUPATION

Occasional typical Late Paleolithic artifacts occur on the surface of much of the area around the small fossil embayment which yielded the human skeleton. In a few places these occur in thin clusters or concentrations, most of which are entirely on the surface and heavily aeolized. There were two dense concentrations, both about 240 m northwest of the

burial and only 45 m apart. Preliminary tests indicated that significant portions of both of these dense clusters were still embedded in the sediments, and merited further investigation. These two areas were named Sites E-81-3 and E-81-4.

Both of these sites were situated on the margin of what was then a small, seasonally flooded embayment which formed at the edge of the floodplain in the area where the shallow basin existed during the Middle Paleolithic. During the early part of the Late Paleolithic occupation in Wadi Kubbaniya, water entered the embayment with the seasonal flood and, during the period of maximum high water, even the dunes surrounding the embayment were inundated. The floor of this small embayment was evidently slightly lower than its mouth, so that a small pool of water was left when the flood receded and fish became trapped in the pool. Fish-bones are very numerous in both of the *in situ* sites, suggesting that it was the fish which attracted the Late Paleolithic groups to this particular spot.

A massive unit of basin silts accumulated in the lower portion of the embayment, while thin lenses of silt interfinger with aeolian sand around the sides, recording a rhythmical, probably annual, cycle of flooding followed by dune migration. The occupations at Site E-81-3 and E-81-4 are embedded within this interfingering silt and sand unit along the edge of the fossil embayment. The lithic assemblages from the sites will be described in detail in the final report on the excavations at Wadi Kubbaniya;

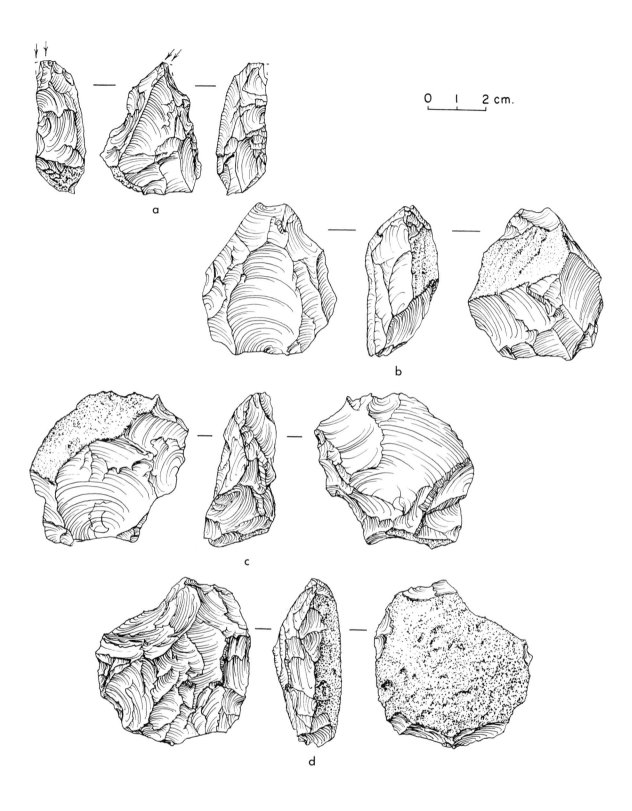

Figure 27. Middle Paleolithic artifacts found on eroded surface of Sand Sheet. a– Burin on denticulate with notch; b–Levallois core; c–partially prepared core; d–unstruck Levallois core.

however, a brief summary of their main features will be useful in placing the Kubbaniya human skeleton in its proper context.

Site E-81-3

This is a small, irregular, ovaloid, surface scatter of lithic artifacts and fossil bone, some 14 m long and 10 m wide. Test excavations indicated that the greatest depth of occupational deposit was near the center of the concentration, where some of the cultural debris had been redeposited in the fill of a shallow swale or peripheral erosional cut, and the remainder occurred in the fill of several small vertical-sided shallow basins, which were probably cultural features or pits. Four distinct horizons of occupation were evident, each occurring on or within a lens of silt and covered by a thin mantle of aeolian sand.

The excavations defined seven features of probable cultural origin: three hearths, two small pits and two larger, oblong pits. The pits were excavated into aeolian sand and filled with reworked silts and sands. The interpretation of them, indeed even their identification as artificial, was complicated by the numerous cycles of lateral erosion and filling, and the many small channels which cut across the site. There are two radiocarbon dates on charcoal from Site E-81-3: the first is 18,120 B.P. ± 670 years (SMU-1036), and the other is 18,360 B.P. ± 790 years (SMU-1129). While consistent, both dates have large standard errors, and both are younger than two dates from Site E-81-4, which is regarded as about the same age or even slightly younger.

The site yielded 17,395 lithic artifacts, of which only 171 are retouched tools. Most of the artifacts were from the excavations: only 1909 of the 17,220 pieces of debitage were from the surface. Most (78%) of the debitage are chips, flakes and blades of quartz. This dominance of the quartz debitage is one of the characteristic features of the assemblage from Site E-81-3. Chert was the next most frequent raw material (1%), followed by basalt (0.5%). Flint, the third most frequent raw material among the retouched tools, is represented in the debitage by only 18 pieces, and there are no flint cores.

The dominance of quartz in the debitage, and the tendency of quartz to fracture into numerous chips or to yield flakes and blades which cannot be identified as to type, distort the frequencies of the debitage classes in the assemblage. A better impression of the lithic technology can be obtained, however, from the frequencies of various debitage types produced in chert. In this raw material, chips are still important (59%), but flakes and blades from single platform cores (17%), and primary flakes and blades (11%) stand out in the remainder of the debitage. Flakes and blades from opposed platform, ninety-degree, and multiple platform cores, occur in that order of importance, but all have frequencies of less than 1% of the chert debitage.

The site yielded 104 cores, of which single platform are the most frequent (36.5%). Core fragments and unidentifiable cores are also important (24%), almost all of quartz. Unpatterned multiple platform cores, again mostly of quartz, are another important group (16.3%). Opposed platform (8.7%), ninety-degree (5.8%), initially struck (5.8%), and discoidal (2.9%) complete the core inventory. As in the debitage, most of the cores are of quartz (53.8%), followed by chert (23.1%), quartzitic sandstone (9.6%), and basalt (8.7%); sandstone and agate are both present but rare. Cortex and *lisse* platforms occur in nearly equal frequencies on the cores (47.4 vs. 45.6%). There are a few with faceted platforms. The backs are rarely prepared extensively; even the single platform variety are mostly unprepared or have only limited preparation.

This simple description conceals some interesting differences between the groups of cores made of quartz and those made of the finer cryptocrystalline materials such as chert and agate. The quartz cores are almost equally divided between the single platform, fragmentary or unidentified, and unpatterned multiple platform varieties. They often have cortex platforms. The chert and agate cores, on the other hand, are mostly single platform and opposed platform types, with nearly equal frequencies for both of these varieties. As in the quartz cores, however, cortex and *lisse* platforms are the most common.

The frequencies of retouched tools by class from Site E-81-3 are recorded in Table 6. Nearly half (47%) of these are of chert, followed by quartz (25%) and flint (15%). Other less frequently used raw materials include basalt, sandstone, quartzitic sandstone and chalcedony. The quartz, basalt and sandstone were used primarily for notches and denticulates, and occasionally for endscrapers.

Backed bladelets are the most frequent tool class (Figure 28). Most of them are made on chert, and all

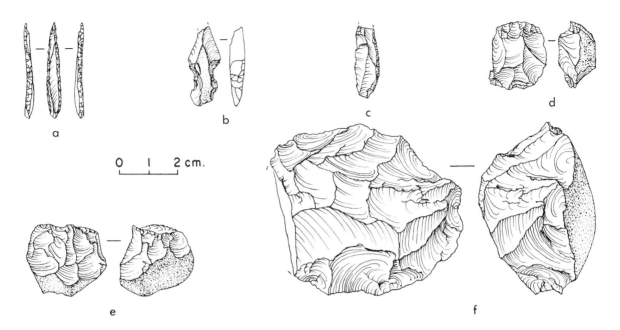

Figure 28. Lithic artifacts from Site E-81-3. a–Double-backed perforator; b–strangled piece; c–retouched piece; d–opposed platform core; e–single platform core; f–unpatterned multiple platform core.

of the identifiable pieces are partially backed with either Ouchtata retouch or obverse backing in nearly equal frequencies. There is a slight preference for the dexter edge, but the distal and proximal sections of the edges are equally popular.

Denticulates, notches and pieces with continuous retouch are also numerically important tool groups. Most of the denticulates and notches are made on quartz and are not well executed. The retouched pieces, on the other hand, are mostly on chert and flint. Endscrapers are also important, and were usually made on thick quartz flakes.

Among the more distinctive tool groups are the double-backed perforators. Most of these have bilateral, obverse backing with the point at the distal end; however, one has obverse retouch on the entire dexter edge and inverse retouch along the entire sinister edge. All are made on chert.

Another important group are the scaled pieces. One of these is made on a chert flake, the remainder are on flint; the bifacially worked edges are usually at the proximal and distal ends.

A single burin, a sidescraper, a composite tool, and two *varia* complete the retouched tool inventory for Site E-81-3. The collection also includes three handstones and a fragment of a possible milling stone. None of the handstones was extensively used

and their identification as grinding implements must be regarded as tentative. A single quartz hammerstone completes the recovered tool kit.

Site E-81-4

About 30 m to the north and along the edge of the same embayment is another dense cluster of lithic artifacts and fossil bones. It was named Site E-81-4.

TABLE 6

Tools from Site E-81-3, Surface and Excavated

Tool Class	No.	%
Endscrapers	7	4.09
Perforators	5	2.92
Burins	1	.58
Backed pieces	46	26.90
Notches	35	20.46
Denticulates	38	22.22
Scaled pieces	5	2.92
Retouched pieces	30	17.54
Sidescrapers	1	.58
Composite tools	1	.58
Varia	2	1.17
Total	171	99.96

It was oval in outline, 11×17 m, with the long axis oriented slightly west of north. Near the center of the concentration was a single hearth, only slightly exposed on the surface, with numerous, small, burned and fossilized fish bones. Excavation disclosed that the hearth was along the edge of a shallow channel filled with alternating lenses of silts and sands and abundant reworked cultural debris.

Except for the hearth, there were no pits or other cultural features. The lithic artifacts, however, are closely similar to those recovered from Site E-81-3, and the two sites are believed to represent occupations by the same or closely similar social units. There are two radiocarbon dates from Site E-81-4: 18,440 B.P. ± 690 years (SMU-1131), and 20,690 B.P. ± 280 years (SMU-1037). Both are on charcoal.

The collection from Site E-81-4 contains 14,361 pieces of debitage. Quartz dominates the raw material utilized at the site, representing 66% of all debitage. The next most frequent raw materials are quartzitic sandstone and chert, each around 10%, followed by basalt and sandstone at 5% each. All other raw materials (agate, flint, chalcedony and petrified wood) occur in amounts of 2% or less.

Except for chips, the most frequent type of debitage is flakes from single platform cores. Unidentified flakes and blades, blades from single platform cores, and primary flakes and blades make up almost all of the remainder of the debitage. Flakes from opposed platform, ninety-degree, or multiple platform cores are present, but rare. The presence of chips and primary flakes from every variety of raw material suggests that some work was done at the site on all of them. On the other hand, among the primary flakes, those on chert are the most frequent followed by quartz, indicating a heavy stress on chert and quartz pebbles from the nearby early Nile gravel terraces.

Only 40 cores were found at Site E-81-4, less than half the number at Site E-81-3. Since the two sites yielded similar quantities of debitage, the relative paucity of cores and the high frequency of primary pieces may indicate that many of the cores were initially exploited at Site E-81-4 and then taken elsewhere before they were exhausted.

Single platform cores are the most frequent (55%), but the collection also includes a few examples of opposed platform, ninety-degree and multiple platform cores. Fragments and initially struck cobbles complete the core group. The most frequent raw material among the cores is chert (42.5%),

closely followed by quartz (32.5%). Basalt and quartzitic sandstone (10% each) and sandstone (5%) were also used. The low frequency of quartz among the cores, in contrast to the dominance of this raw material in the debitage, can perhaps best be explained by the tendency of quartz to fracture into chunks (which would be classified with chips). On the majority of the cores regardless of type, there is no preparation of the back, and only three cores displayed extensive or full preparation. The most frequent platform is cortex (48.4%), followed by *lisse* (38.7%); there are only two cores with faceted platforms.

As a group the cores indicate a simple lithic technology, based on the utilization of stream pebbles. Exploitation was preceded by minimal or no preparation of either the platform or the back, and only rarely was more than one platform or face exploited in the removal of flakes.

Site E-81-4 yielded 189 retouched tools (Figure 29). Their frequencies are given in Table 7. Chert is the preferred raw material (48.1%), followed by quartz (24.3%), agate and basalt (each at 6.9%), flint (4.8%), and quartzitic sandstone (4.2%). Sandstone, petrified wood, and granite were also used, although rarely.

The endscraper group is generally well made and includes eight simple endscrapers (two on flint, one on agate and the remainder on quartz flakes), three denticulated endscrapers (all on quartz flakes), and one endscraper on a notch (also on quartz). The much higher frequency and variety of endscrapers distinguish this assembly from that of Site E-81-3.

The perforator group includes one simple perforator, one perforator on a backed blade, and seven of the double-backed variety, all of which are formed at the distal end with obverse retouch. There is also a simple burin on a break; it is not well struck and may be accidental.

The backed bladelets are the most frequent tool group, but unlike those at Site E-81-3 where only partially backed pieces were represented, the collection includes five arch-ended bladelets (all with obverse retouch), four arch-backed bladelets (two of which have Ouchtata retouch), 17 partially backed bladelets (of which two have Ouchtata retouch and one has inverse backing), eight obtuse-ended bladelets (one with Ouchtata retouch), and 16 fragments of backed bladelets (one with Ouchtata retouch and another with inverse backing). Neither edge was strongly preferred for backing, although the dexter

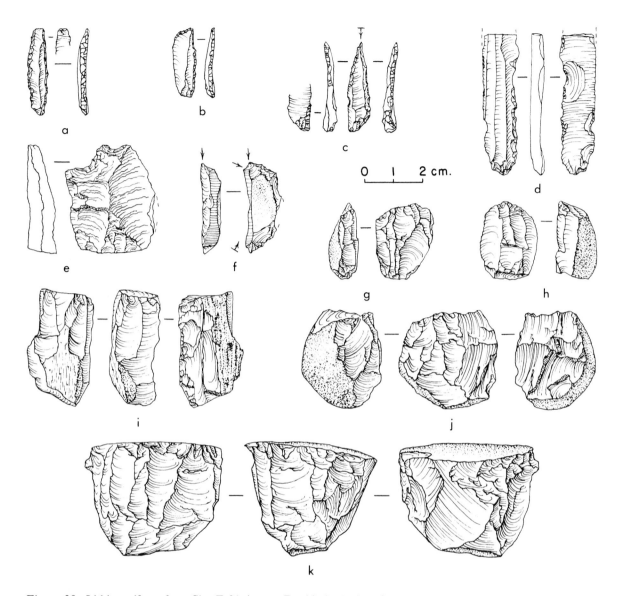

Figure 29. Lithic artifacts from Site E-81-4. a, c–Double-backed perforators; b–backed and truncated bladelet; d–retouched piece; e–denticulate; f–dihedral burin on fragment of endscraper; g, h–opposed platform cores; i, k–single platform cores; j–ninety-degree core.

edge has a slight numerical advantage of 28 to 22. Almost all of the backed pieces are made on chert; there are five of agate and three of flint.

Quartz is the preferred raw material among the notches (17 pieces), closely followed by chert (10 examples). Basalt, quartzitic sandstone and sandstone also were used occasionally. The notches occur on both the sinister and dexter edges, with a slight preference for the dexter edge. There are five pieces notched at the distal end. Retouched notches are over twice as frequent as those produced by a

single blow and the retouch (or blow) is inverse or obverse in nearly equal frequencies. There was no strong raw material preference for the denticulates. Quartz and basalt were the most frequent (five examples each), closely followed by quartzitic sandstone (three pieces). There are two denticulates of flint and one each of granite and sandstone. Surprisingly, there are no chert denticulates. The denticulation occurs most frequently on the sinister edge (10 examples), with the dexter (three), bilateral (two), and distal (two) edges used only

TABLE 7

Retouched Tools by Class from Site E-81-4,
Surface and Excavated

Type	No.	%
Endscrapers	12	6.3
Perforators	9	4.8
Burins	1	.5
Backed pieces	50	26.5
Notches	35	18.5
Denticulates	17	9.0
Truncations	4	2.1
Scaled pieces	23	12.2
Retouched pieces	28	14.8
Sidescrapers	2	1.1
Varia	8	4.2
Total	189	100.0

occasionally. Most (13) of the denticulations are formed by obverse retouch and usually by a single blow (12 examples).

The few truncations are all simple. Three are distal and sinister (one is on a core-trimming element), and the fourth is proximal and dexter.

Scaled pieces are another important tool type at Site E-81-4. Most (12) are made on chert, with quartz (five) and agate (four) also common. This contrasts with the emphasis on flint for the scaled pieces at Site E-81-3. The bifacial scaled retouch usually occurs at the proximal and distal ends of the flakes, but on a few of the pieces the retouch is unifacial and on alternate faces at the battered ends. The *varia* include four battered quartz and quartizitic sandstone flakes which could be classified as scaled pieces.

Almost all (23) of the pieces with continuous retouch have obverse retouch, but its placement is highly variable. Nearly a third are retouched on the sinister edge; the remainder are divided between dexter, distal and bilateral, or the edge is unknown. Most (16) are on chert, but quartz was also frequently used (six). The remainder are of flint (two), petrified wood, agate, basalt and sandstone (one each).

The two sidescrapers are made on thick flakes, one chert and the other basalt. On the chert piece, the retouched dexter edge is straight and well executed, while the basalt example is an atypical convergent sidescraper on a possible core-trimming element.

The remainder of the tool kit consists of two hammerstones (one quartz and one sandstone), four fragments of slightly used handstones (all of sandstone), and a large sandstone slab, somewhat abraded on one face. This last piece may have been used as an anvil or a milling stone.

Artifacts with the Skeleton, Site E-82-6

During the removal of the calcareous matrix from around the human skeleton, two fragments of bladelets from opposed platform cores were found in the forepart of the left abdominal region (Figure 30). Since the body had been placed in the grave-pit face downward, it is very likely that the bladelets were contemporaneous with the burial and not a later admixture. They are, therefore, probably among the best evidence available for the age of the skeleton and strongly indicate that it is not Middle Paleolithic in age as was originally thought.

It is not certain how the bladelets came to be inside the abdominal region. It is possible that they were in some sort of container which was carried over the abdomen and that they were pressed into the cavity with decomposition of the softer body parts. An alternative explanation, and one favored by these writers, is that they were parts of a projectile, perhaps the lateral barbs, which caused the death of the individual. Either of the pieces could also have served as the distal end of a projectile; the distal end need not have been pointed, since it could have been sufficiently sharp, even though rounded, to serve as an effective weapon. There are many ethnographic examples of unpointed projectile tips. Blunt tips (although not bladelets) also occur frequently on Old Kingdom and later Egyptian arrows.

One of the bladelets is made of chalcedony and the other is made of chert. Both raw materials are identical in color and quality to those commonly used by the Late Paleolithic inhabitants of Wadi Kubbaniya. They occur as small cobbles in the gravel beds on the sandstone scarp along the lower portion of the wadi.

The bladelets are broken and their original shape cannot be exactly reconstructed. One (Figure 30:b) may be classified as a partially retouched Ouchtata bladelet; the retouch occurs along the mid-portion of the dexter edge. The other bladelet is not retouched.

Similar bladelets occur throughout the Kubbaniya Late Paleolithic sequence, but they are most

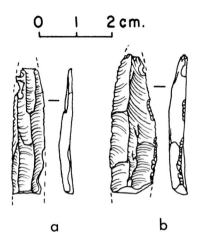

Figure 30. Bladelets found inside abdominal cavity of the Kubbaniya skeleton (Site E-82-6). a–Unretouched chalcedony bladelet; b–chert bladelet with partial Ouchtata retouch.

common in the Kubbaniyan itself, both in its early (or Fakhurian) phase and in the main Kubbaniyan occupation, or from *ca.* 21,000 to *ca.* 17,000 B.P. However, the geological evidence discussed above indicates a slightly greater antiquity for the skeleton.

Discussion of Late Paleolithic Sites

Several Late Paleolithic taxonomic entities occur in Wadi Kubbaniya. Most of them are found in the massive dune/silt remnant some 3 km up the wadi from Sites E-81-3 and E-81-4. The best known industry from this area is the Kubbaniyan, characterized by high frequencies (up to 80% of all retouched tools) of Ouchtata bladelets and scaled pieces, and rare but well made burins (Wendorf *et al.* 1980). Numerous radiocarbon dates place the Kubbaniyan between 18,600 and 17,000 B.P.

Several other sites with a related but significantly different lithic industry stratigraphically precede the Kubbaniyan in the same area. These sites, sometimes informally referred to as "Early Kubbaniyan", are characterized by an emphasis on quartz for raw material, a moderate stress on backed bladelets (as opposed to Ouchtata bladelets), the consistent presence of perforators, and slightly higher frequencies of both notches and denticulates. These are precisely the features found at Sites E-81-3 and E-81-4.

Three of the "Early Kubbaniyan" sites in the area of the extensive dune/silt remnant were excavated, two of them extensively (E-81-6 and E-82-3). There are four dates on charcoal from these sites: 18,010 B.P. ± 340 years (SMU-1033), regarded as too recent because several stratigraphically higher sites have older dates; 19,340 B.P. ± 370 years (SMU-1033; a second count on the same sample as that cited above); 19,030 B.P. ± 180 years (SMU-1157), all from Site E-81-6; and 19,810 B.P. ± 310 years (SMU-1136) from Site E-82-3, stratigraphically the oldest site in the group.

Sites E-81-3 and E-81-4, although near the mouth of the wadi, are at about the same elevation as Sites E-81-6 and E-82-3, that is, between 106 and 107 m above sea level, and thus all were probably inundated by the seasonal floods at about the same time. In any case, there is no stratigraphic basis for an earlier age for the sites near the mouth of the wadi: the sites near the mouth of the wadi (E-81-3 and E-81-4) and the two sites located farther up the wadi (E-81-6 and E-82-3) could well be generally about the same age, with Site E-82-3 being slightly older. Although there are three dates younger than 18,500 B.P., the probable time range for the entire "Early Kubbaniyan" group is from *ca.* 21,000 to 19,000 B.P.

The three dates younger than 18,500 B.P., which conflict with several dates around 18,500 B.P. from sites more recent than the Early Kubbaniyan group can perhaps be best explained as due to contamination by more slightly recent humates. The charcoal in all of the Kubbaniya sites is only partially carbonized and it requires special pretreatment procedures. It is possible, therefore, that not all of the humate portion was removed from those samples, with the result that the dates are slightly too young.

The "Early Kubbaniyan" has some general resemblances to the Fakhurian, an industry previously known only at five sites near Esna, about 150 km downstream from Wadi Kubbaniya (Lubell 1974). There are two radiocarbon dates from the Fakhurian of 18,020 B.P. ± 330 years (I-3416) and 17,590 B.P. ± 300 years (I-3415), both on *Unio* shells. These are slightly younger than the indicated age for the Early Kubbaniyan, but this may be related to the material dated (*Unio* may not be as reliable as charcoal), or the Fakhurian sites may indeed be slightly younger. In any case, both the Fakhurian and the Early Kubbaniyan are characterized by four major tool classes: backed bladelets, perforators, retouched pieces, and notched or denticulated pieces. There are, however, important differences in technology. The Fakhurian has a much greater emphasis on opposed platform and ninety-degree cores, and there is frequent use of the bipolar technique. Whether these differences are sufficient to warrant a separate classification of the two is not yet clear. At present, it seems equally appropriate either to group the two together into a single entity, the Fakhurian, or to view these early Late Paleolithic sites as the earliest expression of the Kubbaniyan industry, the entity which was present less than 1,500 years later, from about 18,500 to 17,000 B.P.

CHAPTER 4

DESCRIPTION OF THE HUMAN SKELETON

Cleaning and Casting of the Skeleton

by

T. D. Stewart and Michael Tiffany

Introduction

Early in 1982, when Dr. Wendorf found an apparently ancient human burial in Wadi Kubbaniya on the west side of the upper Nile Valley, he asked one of us (T.D.S.) to describe the skeleton. After the offer had been accepted, negotiations were carried out between the Egyptian authorities and the U.S. Embassy in Cairo (representing the Smithsonian Institution and Southern Methodist University) for most of a year before the skeleton was released and reached Washington. Because most of the skeleton was embedded in a block of consolidated sand, the work of exposing and removing the bones was not done in the Anthropology Department of the Smithsonian Institution, but in the Preparation Laboratory of the Department of Vertebrate Paleontology (by M.T., who also made the casts of the bones). This arrangement proved very fortunate since T.D.S. was hospitalized late in 1983 and was not in proper physical condition to study the original bones before their return to Egypt in April, 1984. Happily, Dr. J. Lawrence Angel, his replacement as Curator of Physical Anthropology, undertook the detailed study (see below).

As removed from the packing-box in Washington, the Kubbaniya skeleton was found to consist of three main parts: a block of consolidated sand (approximately 60 cm long, 45 cm wide and 15 cm high), with most of the bones embedded in it; pieces of matrix-covered skull and lower jaw with the first three cervical vertebrae attached to the skull base; and assorted small pieces of bone, mainly parts of the upper and lower extremities.

Skull and Lower Jaw

Since the best evidence for human physical type is provided by the head, the first restoration effort was directed there. The matrix was cleaned away from the external surfaces of the facial areas, and the entire remaining face restored (Figure 31). Obviously missing are all of the vault posterior to the vertical plane through the left external auditory meatus, much of the right temporal bone and zygomatic arch (Figure 32), the posterior borders of the frontal bone and part of the anterior border of the foramen magnum. However, enough of the basilar part of the occipital bone is preserved to show that the spheno-occipital synchondrosis is closed, and therefore that this individual was more than 20 years old at death (McKern and Stewart 1957:Table 15).

There was a corresponding loss of bone on the right side of the lower jaw, consisting in particular of the whole ascending ramus behind the right M_3 (Figure 32). By contrast, bone loss on the left side of the lower jaw, which was most probably accidental, was confined to the horizontal ramus, from M_2 and M_3 down to the lower border between the chin and the beginning point of the ascending ramus (Figures 31 and 33). Bone loss in the rest of the facial area was not extensive, largely because the teeth were in edge-to-edge bite and normal occlusion and were held together by the consolidated sand.

The Endocranial Cavity

The removal of the sandy matrix from the anterior portion of the endocranial cavity permitted a cast to be made of that area (Figure 34). This cast provides additional evidence that the restoration of the frontal bone is accurate and that the whole vault had been elongated in shape (perhaps dolichocranic or nearly so). At this stage of work, it was also increasingly clear that the wind damage to the skull was not only to the posterior parts, but more to the right than the left side.

49

Figure 31. Surviving portion of skull (approximately one-third) seen from left side in Frankfort position.

Relation of Skull to Top of Block

One of the first steps taken in preparing the external surfaces of the skull for restoration was the removal of the fragments of upper cervical vertebrae, which had been attached to the occipital bone by matrix. The reassembling and identification of these fragments was one of the first tasks connected with the cleaning of the bones exposed on the upper surface of the block. It eventually became evident that the whole vertebral column was represented, although not by complete segments since the originally exposed topmost parts, especially the vertebral spinous processes, laminae and transverse processes, had been destroyed by erosion (Figure 35). Seven cervical, twelve thoracic and five lumbar vertebrae, the normal complement, were present. It was later found that only a portion of the first sacral vertebra remained, and that the vertebral or posterior ends of the ribs and the bodies, or wings, of the scapulae had also been destroyed.

The Leg Fragments

The leg bone fragments, like the skull fragments, were shipped from Egypt unattached to the major part of the skeleton. There were about 174 of them, slender in shape, polished and rarely exceeding 5 cm in length. Almost none of the longbone fragments could be assigned to a specific bone, all being cortical bone (Figure 36). The few identifiable exceptions were all from the left side. They comprise the distal end of the femur, the patella, the distal end of the tibia and the talus. The only part not recovered outside the block was a portion of the head of the femur, which was found still in the acetabulum of the pelvis when the removal of the matrix from the under side of the block reached this stage (Figure 37). The finding of three left wrist bones (navicular, capitate and lunate), two left middle phalanges (II and III) and two left distal phalanges (II and IV) should also be mentioned. No part of the right hand was present.

Figure 32. Basal view of skull vault and superior view of lower jaw showing tooth-wear was greatest anteriorly.

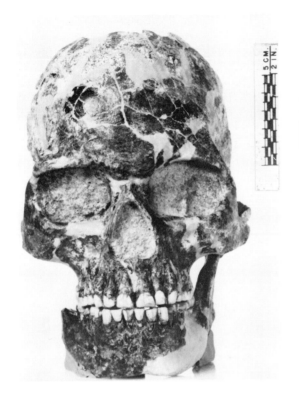

Figure 33. Front view of skull in Frankfort position. Edge-to-edge occlusion of teeth is as found; matrix not cleared from nasal and orbital cavities.

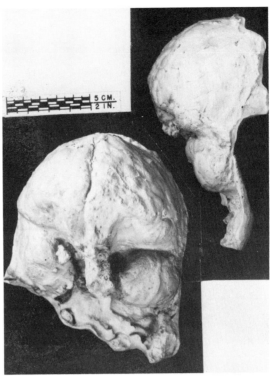

Figure 34. Front and side views of endocranial cast. (Matrix not cleared from orbital cavities.)

Bone Surfaces on Lower Side of Block

Since nothing more could be learned about the bones exposed on the top surface of the block until the rest of their surfaces were freed from the adherent matrix, M.T. made a cast of the top surface (Figure 35) and then turned the block over. When the matrix had been removed, the most notable aspect was the complete lack of surface damage, owing to the protection from sandblasting the face-down burial afforded (Figure 38). The arms, extended along the sides of the pelvis, had reached beyond the edge of the block, so both hands had been detached as had also the distal ends of the right radius and ulna. By contrast, the left forearm bones, although broken distally in several places could be fully restored (Figure 41). At the conclusion of the restoration process, therefore, the three left arm bones were complete, but on the right only the humerus was complete. It is also worthy of note that the thoraco-lumbar vertebral column came out of its matrix in one piece and with most of the rib heads

attached. This revealed that the shape of the spinal curvature had been retained even after the great number of years the body had been in the prone position (Figure 39). The surviving parts of the pelvis were removed at the same time as the thoraco-lumbar column. The natural relationship between what was left of the two innominates and the sacrum had been maintained up to this point by the matrix (Figure 42). M.T. now connected them securely by brass rods so as not to lose this relationship, even in the casting.

Additional Comments

Since the authors of this section are primarily physical anthropologists and lack field experience in the area of the Upper Nile Valley, we do not feel qualified to evaluate all of the findings connected with the skeleton. Two of them have already been mentioned: the face-down mode of burial and the fragmentation of the leg bones. The third was two

Figure 35. Top surface of block after cleaning matrix from uppermost surfaces of bones. Note extensive erosion of bones and exposure of bladelet between T12 on left and rib ends on right.

Figure 36. Sand-blasted fragments of longbone cortex (35 out of 174) found outside burial-block.

bladelets, one of chalcedony and one of chert, found at two different points between the lowermost ribs and the lumbar vertebrae, during the removal of the consolidated sand filling the forepart of the left abdominal region (Figures 30, 35, 38 and 40; see also Chapter 3). The locations of the bladelets were close enough to the injuries seen at the distal ends of the right ulna and left humerus to suggest to us that these bladelets, too, represent injuries, and may even have been the cause of death. Actual proof of this is lacking, as is proof of the alternate explanation that the bladelets were simply contained in a pouch attached to a belt worn by this individual.

It is possible that these three findings might be related, since the burial was single, isolated and not part of a cemetery. Although Wendorf believes that the breaks result from natural erosional processes with possible accidental damage by animals (cf. Wendorf and Schild 1980:Fig. 2.44 – *ed.*), we are not convinced that this was the case at Kubbaniya.

Figure 37. Under-surface of the pelvis still embedded in block after removal of matrix. Note part of head of left femur still in place in acetabulum.

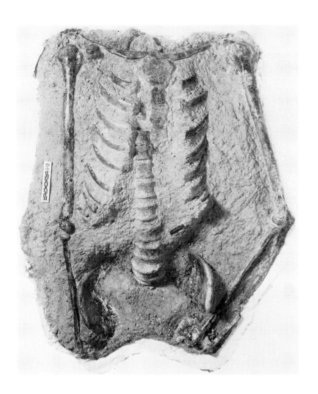

Figure 38. Exposure of bone surfaces on lower side of block after removal of matrix.

Figure 39. Right side of supra-sacral vertebral column as removed from block, showing retention of curvature.

Also, we do not know how widely scattered the human leg bone fragments were at Kubbaniya at the time of their recovery. Here too, then, proof is lacking and the breaks might have been produced deliberately by the buried individual's human enemies. (See, however, Chapter 5–*ed.*)

DESCRIPTION AND COMPARISON
OF THE SKELETON

by

J. Lawrence Angel and Jennifer Olsen Kelley

After T.D.S. and M.T. had cleaned and mended the Wadi Kubbaniya skull and skeleton, and M.T. had made exact plastic replicas as described above, J.L.A. undertook study of this Upper Paleolithic male in early 1984, at the request of T.D.S. who was recovering from an ophthalmic infection. J.O.K. worked with J.L.A. in this thorough examination of and report on the remains; the skeleton, skull, vertebrae and left hand were measured between February 10 and 17 1984. J.L.A. then completed detailed photography, including standard views of skull, teeth, pelvis, vertebral columnm, long bones, right shoulder, asymmetries, left hand, healed right ulna parry-fracture and left lateral epicondylar wound with embedded point (Figures 41–52).

Our overall impression is of a young man, muscular but not massive or very tall, a strong right-handed thrower (of spear or javelin?) with asymmetries fitting this activity. In childhood he was well-nourished. An old, healed parry-fracture of the right

Figure 40. Detail of bladelet resting against bodies of second and third lumbar vertebrae.

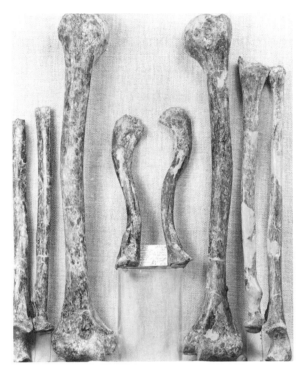

Figure 41. Long bones of upper extremities. Note greater robusticity and muscle markings of right side.

Figure 42. Left innominate, showing striking projection of anterior superior spine, strong inferior spine and supra-acetabular groove (for hip flexion and knee extension).

forearm and a chip of flint or chalcedony broken off in the left humerus' crest for extensor muscles of the hand only days or weeks before death fit the kind of interpersonal violence seen later at Jebel Sahaba (Wendorf 1968a). Two bladelets of chalcedony and of chert inside the lower abdomen between left lower ribs and lumbar vertebrae are evidence of the probably violent cause of death. The man's build, facial features and specific genetic traits (e.g. wrinkling of third molar crowns) lie close to the central values of the Jebel Sahaba population, which was apparently directly ancestral to modern Nubians and Sudanese.

Detailed observations and evidence for these and other inferences follow.

Sex Criteria

These are clearly male. They include a fairly low brim/posterior (cheilotic) index (*ca.* 74), fairly large heads of femur (48 mm) and humerus (almost 48 mm), straight humero-ulnar carrying angle (175°) of upper extremity, adequately broad shoulders compared to hips (breadths relative to stature 21.7% and 16.0% (?), above-average degree of muscularity and extreme (+++) development of browridges (Figures 31–33 and 41).

Age Criteria

Epiphyseal closure is complete except for medial clavicles and heads of ribs. Pubic symphysis developmental phase is between 2 and 3. The iliac crest is fused anteriorly but shows a line of fusion posteriorly. Tooth eruption is complete, with upper third molars showing less wear than lower M_3s and hence only recently at occlusal level. Coronal suture shows beginning closure. Age, therefore, is between 20 and 25, or about 23 years by current standards (Stewart 1979).

Figure 43. Upper three thoracic vertebrae with ribs 1 and 2 (ribs set too horizontally in photograph).

Race Criteria

Relatively long forearms (Brachial index 79), short lumbar region and trunk, considerable prognathism (face profile angle 75°, alveolar angle 52° and chin profile angle 106°), low and broad nose with slight subnasal grooves, slight inversion of jaw ramus above the slight gonial flare, and + degree wrinkling of third molars all fit with modern U.S. Blacks—i.e. mainly African recent hybrids (Figures 31, 33 and 53). However, the face looks quite Australoid and not dissimilar to European Upper Paleolithic types (Predmost), while the sum total of proportions and single traits are very much closer to typical features of the Jebel Sahaba Nubians (Anderson 1968) than to any other group. These similarities will be discussed later.

Stature and Build

Because of the above comparisons, clarified metrically in Tables 8 and 9, we used Trotter's and Gleser's (1958) stature estimation formulae for Negro males. From lengths of humerus, radius, and ulna the stature is 172.18 cm with a 3–4 cm error of estimate. As a test, we compared the bones with a Terry Collection Black male (#204) of the same age and stature. The results substantiate the similarity in proportions although not at all in face (Figure 53), in hand (Figure 47) or, probably, in pelvis.

Body build is (probably) slender, with short trunk (relative sitting height only *ca.* 47%), below average shoulder breadth (clavi-humeral index 45 and actual biacromial living estimate 370 to 375), average hip breadth (relative bi-iliac 16) as in the modern U.S. Blacks "accidental-death" sample (Table 8) and probably smallish thorax. The Wadi Kubbaniya man was right-handed, as is seen in level of the posterior border of glenoid surface of right scapula (Stewart 1980) and in the usual asymmetries (longer humerus, shorter right clavicle). Humerus and radius shaft thicknesses and elbow breadths are just below modern averages, femur shaft cortical thickness (on a probable mid-shaft fragment) is 8 mm, and muscle ridges overall are average. Build is not in any way massive and in life this man presumably had the high surface:mass ratio expected in a heat-adapted hunter or fisherman (Figures 41–48).

Nutrition and Health

We have not yet arranged for study of bone chemistry. Bone strontium values would tell us nothing without analyses of both the actual herbivores eaten vs. the carnivores, and soil strontium (Bisel 1980;

TABLE 8

Comparative Measurements of Male Skeletons

	Upper Paleolithic					Modern				
	Jebel Sahaba (Site 117)		Wadi Kubban-iya	Taforalt		U.S. White		U.S. Black		Martin's Number
	M	N		M	N	M	N	M	N	
Measurements (mm)										
Stature (cm)	172.8	9	172.2	176.6	15	174.2	93	171.2	32	
Humerus, max. length	328.7	3	333−	336.0	18	330.6	64	329.0	25	1
Humerus, max. head diameter	47	1	47+	48.7	16	49.3	63	46.7	24	9
Midshaft, maximum			22	23.7	19	24.0	69	23.9	25	5
Diameter, minimum			19	18.4	19	19.1	72	19.7	25	6
Bi-epicondylar breadth			63	66.3	20	64.1	62	64.0	24	4
Clavicle, max. length	161	1	151	159.3	11	153.6	55	154.8	20	1
Radius, max. length	274.0	4	261	266.8	13	247.8	56	260.6	20	1
Ulna, max. length	293.8	6	286	288.2	16	267.8	54	278.9	22	1
Femur, max. head diameter	46.2	12	48	51.6	15	48.8	72	46.7	27	18
Lumbar, anterior heights			127	144.7	3	144.7	53	137.3	25	1
Talus groove-head length			48?	54.7	18	56.4	46	54.3	20	1
Indices										
Relative to stature:										
Sitting height			(47.2)	(51.1)	*	52.1	37	49.8	14	
Bi-iliac breadth			16.0??			17.2	55	16.0	26	
Pelvic brim index[1]			100?			91.9	59	92.5	25	
Iliac brim segment			74.3??			73.9	66	69.6	26	
Lumbar curve[2]			104.7	101.6	4	97.6	47	98.1	22	
Brachial[3]	83.4	*	78.8	79.1	*	75.3	61	78.4	25	
Clavi-humeral[4]	49.0	*	45.4	47.4	*	46.5	61	46.5	24	
Crural[5]	86.1	*	(high)	83.6	*	82.3	62	84.8	26	
Humerus, midshaft[6]			86.1	77.7	19	80.0	81	82.4	30	
Humerus, robusticity			12.3	12.5	*	13.0	*	13.2	*	
Talus, height/length			56.2	55.7	17	56.9	54	58.7	20	

[1](a-p) × 100/transverse   [3]Radius × 100/humerus   [5]Tibia × 100/femur
[2]Posterior × 100/anterior   [4]Clavicle × 100/humerus   [6]Minimum × 100/maximum

Sillen 1981). Bone zinc might indicate both meat and fish protein (Bisel 1980; Yesner 1980); many fish bones occur in Kubbaniyan sites, perhaps meaning that less red meat was consumed than at other Upper Paleolithic sites.

Morphological evidence on nutritional health is mixed. Skull base height (Angel 1982) at just over 19 mm (?), like that of modern U.S. Blacks, is up to one standard deviation below that of pre-farming meat-eating hunters; it may mean only a slight inadequacy of maternal milk—there are no tooth enamel arrest lines signalling weaning disturbance (Cook and Buikstra 1979; Sillen and Smith 1984). To the extent that T.D.S. and M.T. could restore the pelvic inlet (Figure 42), its index (*ca.* 100) suggests very good later childhood nutrition (Angel 1982; Angel and Kelly 1984), which is in accord with the lack of hypoplastic growth-arrest lines on tooth enamel and the very healthy teeth. However, the below-average stature (by hunting period standards) may mean adolescent stress from some lack of calories and certainly from fighting. The old parry-

TABLE 9

Comparative Measurements and Indices of Male Skulls

	Upper Paleolithic							Modern				Definitions	
	Jebel Sahaba (Site 117)		Wadi Kubbaniya	Afalou, Mechta		Taforalt		U.S. White		U.S. Black		Martin's Number	Biometric Number
	M	N		M	N	M	N	M	N	M	N		
Age at death	36	20	23 ca.	34	21	32	47	42.4	125	40.0	45		
Measurements (mm)													
Vault length	194.8	15	(186)	194.6	29	194.6	14	187.1	107	187.2	40	1	L
Maximum breadth	137.0	14	(134)	145.3	30	146.1	14	142.9	108	138.2	40	8	B
Basion–bregma height	132.5	9	132	143.9	15	144.0	7	139.4	100	135.6	38	17	H'
Auricular–vertex height	112.7	11	109+	122.0	27	119.3	14	119.5	104	117.5	38	(21)	(OH)
Base height	20.8	9	19+	23.2	15	25.7	7	21.3	99	19.3	38	17–21*	
Base length	100.2	9	95	108.7	15	108.7	7	103.7	100	102.6	38	5	LB
Face length	104.5	7	103	101.3	15	104.3	6	96.6	66	103.4	31	40	GL
Minimum frontal breadth	101.6	13	92	98.5	28	94.0	13	96.8	107	97.4	40	9	B'
Bizygomatic breadth	142.1	8	137?	141.4	26	147.4	8	131.1	99	131.1	39	45	J
Bigonial breadth	101.9	13	99?	111.0	16	113.7	10	100.0	78	96.9	30	66	wz
Chin height	39.7	16	32+	40.1	17	39.8	12	34.1	65	36.9	28	69	h'
Total face height	120.6	14	105	120.7	16	123.4	*	121.7	55	124.1	27	47	GH
Upper face height	70.8	13	68	70.3	26	68.6	11	72.8	75	72.0	32	48	G'H
Nose height	46.7	11	44	52.9	24	54.0	10	52.5	94	50.4	38	55	NH
Nose breadth	28.1	9	27	28.3	28	28.5	9	23.9	93	26.1	39	54	NB
Orbit height	31.2	14	30+	31.2	25	31.6	7	33.7	93	34.5	39	52	O2'
Orbit breadth	43.9	14	46	*40.4	23	44.2	9	40.4	93	40.4	39	51	O1'
Alveolar length	60.1	8	64	58.4	16	58.4	4	53.0	65	57.8	33	60	G1'
Palatal breadth	68.6	13	66	70.5	17	71.3	6	63.5	66	66.9	31	61	EB
Minimum ramus breadth	43.3	15	37	34.2	18	40.3	12	30.2	83	34.2	30	71	rb'
Jaw angle			116	118.8	18	113.0	11	127.5	79	124.2	29	79	m∠
Face profile			75	89.4	23	85.3	9	87.5	70	81.1	31	72	P∠

TABLE 9—*Continued*

	Upper Paleolithic								Modern				Definitions
	Jebel Sahaba (Site 117)		Wadi Kubbaniya		Afalou, Mechta		Taforalt		U.S. White		U.S. Black		Martin's Number
	M	N	M	N	M	N	M	N	M	N	M	N	
Age at death	36	20	23 *ca.*		34	21	32	47	42.4	125	40.0	45	
Indices													
Cranial	70.3	14	(72)		74.6	30	74.5	13	76.5	107	73.9	49	8 × 100/1
Auricular height	67.9	*	(68.1)		71.8	*	70.1	13	72.4	104	72.2	37	(21) × 200/L+8
Fronto-parietal height	74.2	*	(68.7)		68.0	27	64.3	*	67.8	107	70.6	40	9 × 100/8
Cranio-facial	103.7	*	(102.2)		97.4	23	100.9	*	91.8	100	94.8	39	45 × 100/8
Fronto-gonial	108.2		107.6		115.0	12	121.0	*	103.1	69	99.8	27	66 × 100/9
Facial	84.8	7	76.6		87.2	16	83.7	8	92.8	55	94.0	26	47 × 100/45
Upper facial	50.3	6	45.3?		49.7	26	46.4	7	55.5	72	55.2	33	48 × 100/45
Nasal	59.7	8	61.4		53.6	24	52.1	6	45.7	93	51.9	38	54 × 100/55
Orbital	71.1	13	66.7		77.2	*	71.1	5	83.4	93	85.4	39	52 × 100/51a
Alveolar-palatal	112.1	7	103.1		122.0	15	122.2	5	120.4	63	115.4	30	61 × 100/60
Gnathic	103.2	7	108.4		94.2	15	98.0		92.2	66	101.0	31	40 × 100/5
σ ratio, variability	111.3	11			95	21	100 *ca.*		106.1	91	112.5	36	σ × 100/standard σ

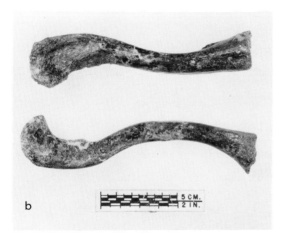

Figure 44. a – Manubrium; b – clavicles; c – body of sternum.

fracture of the lower third of the right ulna shows enough sub-periosteal thickening and smooth re-modelling of callus to have occurred at about age 15 (Figure 51); it shows a little dorsolateral deviation and 2–3 mm thickening (15×17 mm as opposed to 12×14 mm on the left at this level). This fighting points to psychological stress, with this factor rather than disease limiting general health.

The skull vault lacks the thickened diploë of anaemia (Angel 1984) and the teeth suggest that there were no serious childhood diseases (Figures 31–33).

Teeth

The overall health of the dentition (Figure 32) shows a lack of any lesions (no caries, loss, or abscesses), with a trace of alveolar bone absorption and only slight periodontal disease. Bite is edge-to-edge and occlusion normal. A slight trema (gap) occurs between upper median incisors. Tooth wear is medium except for marked wear on incisors, and slight wear on third molars, allowing wrinkling to be visible. Incisors are very slightly crowded and the upper right lateral incisor rotated 70°. Molar cusps are 4-4-4 upper and 5-4-5 lower. Upper incisors show slight shoveling but no labial tubercles; and carabelli cusps and protostylid pits are also absent. Lower premolars are large as are molar crowns—very similar to the Jebel Sahaba teeth (Butler 1968).

Way of Life

All the lumbar vertebrae show slight bilateral concavities in the posterior third of upper and lower disk surfaces: incipient Scheuermann's "disease" probably from sudden lifting and carrying game or netted fish (Figure 49). Both humeri show striking bowing, almost sigmoid, in part linked with deltoid muscle pull—though deltoid and pectoral crests are still average (this is, after all, quite a young man) except for extra cresting on the right humerus (Figure 41). The right shoulder joint is larger than the left (humerus heads: 49+ vs. 45+ mm; glenoid surfaces: 42×31 vs. 41×28 mm), and directed more backward (torsion angle 49° vs. 37° on left); both humeri have the greater tuberosities placed more cranially than usual and strong markings for insertion of all rotator cuff muscles (teres minor, infraspinatus, supraspinatus and subscapularis). Both acromion processes are large (53+?×27 mm right a-p×tranverse and 54×24 left). Both clavicles are wide and thick at their acromial or distal ends (30×12 right and 26×11 mm left), have strong markings for the pairs of coraco-clavicular ligaments, and strong fossae for costo-clavicular ligaments. The right fossa is huge—18×10×6 mm—and there is a very deep groove for subclavius muscle insertion (Figure 44:b). On the stout manubrium (Figure 44:a), the right pressure joint for the medial clavicle disks is larger (29×33 mm) and less transverse than the left pressure joint (22×19 mm). The upper three ribs (lower incomplete) have marked tubercles for the origin of the upper section

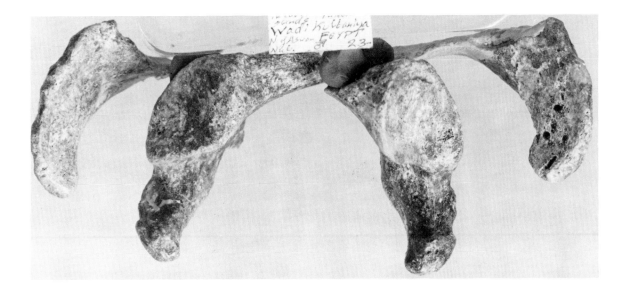

Figure 45. Scapulae (lateral). Right one is 8% larger than left.

of serratus anterior, the deepest pushing, striking and throwing muscle. (Anyone who has had rib fractures will recall vividly that he could neither push open a door, nor throw, using the scapula on the injured side, until at least the fibrous bony union was firm.) These observations show that the shoulder and arm regions of the Wadi Kubbaniya man were very well developed for throwing and thrusting, especially with the right hand.

In the lower parts of the arm (Figures 46 and 47), as expected, the right biepicondylar breadth is 65+ mm vs. 60 mm on the left, and right radial head diameter is 23 mm vs. 22 mm on the left. However, the strong supinator crest on the right ulna (that on the left is of average size) is more critical. When the elbow is flexed at 90°, the biceps is the muscle which supinates powerfully (as in twisting a doorknob or in driving a right-threaded screw), but as the elbow is straightened it is the less strongly placed supinator which twists the radius while tying it tightly into the radio-humeral-ulnar joint. Kennedy (1983) found large supinator crests on the throwing arms of a baseball pitcher and of latest Paleolithic hunters in northern India, while Kelley and Angel (1983) have observed them in eighteenth to early nineteenth century iron-worker slaves at Catoctin, Maryland, who manipulated hot iron bars, raked crude ore from bands and chopped down the trees needed for charcoal. We believe that Anderson's observation (1968:1023) about the ulna: "The interosseous border, like that of the radius, is very sharp and projects laterally in its upper half" refers to a strong supinator crest in the apparently spear-using Jebel Sahaba people.

Anderson's further findings of a striking above-wrist ridge for pronator quadratus plus radial angulation of distal ulna also fit the Wadi Kubbaniya man. This muscle ties together the two forearm bones for the stress and then recoil of throwing, of coal-mining with a jackhammer, and other *sudden* stress. The Kubbaniya man was clearly a right-handed spear-thrower in hunting and probably fishing, according to the preceding observations. He was probably also strong in hand-to-hand combat with hostile groups.

The left hand (Figures 46 and 47) is rather small (189×64 mm reconstructed) with metacarpal II length *ca.* 67 mm compared with a mean for U.S. Black males of 72.7 mm; although navicular at 39×17?×(12), capitate at 34+×16×(22) and hamate at 20×16×(22+) are average to large. Metacarpal tubercles for the fanlike collateral ligaments at knuckles are sharp and the dorsal tubercles on middle and distal phalanges between and in the extensor tendons (from interossei) are pointed. However, the crests for the vaginal ligaments holding the flexor tendon sheaths are only average: this is a wiry hand for strong and delicate work rather than heavy gripping. It is the hand of a fisher or hunter (and perhaps also maker of nets and blades) rather

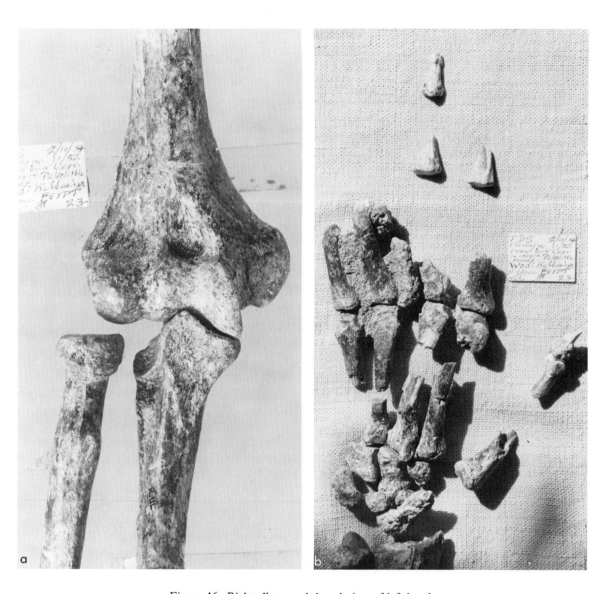

Figure 46. Right elbow and dorsal view of left hand.

than of a farmer or smith or miner. We assume that the right hand (missing *post-mortem*) was similar, but stronger.

Cause of Death

Two tapering bladelets of chert and chalcedony were found, respectively, pointing down on the left side of the lumbar 2 and 3 vertebral bodies and pointing diagonally upward to T^{12} and next to ribs 10 and 11 (Figure 40). There is no probable way in which the bladelets could have sifted past the ribs and lumbar transverse processes from the earth covering the face-down burial. The most logical explanation is that enemies speared this man from behind. The chalcedony bladelet lay in the position of the abdominal aorta and the chert bladelet lay near the position of the left kidney and aorta; either could have caused a fatal haemorrhage. His left elbow may not have recovered completely from the spear which left its broken stone tip in the lateral epicondylar ridge (Figure 52); this tip is not a fragment of either of the blades in the abdomen (Figure 30).

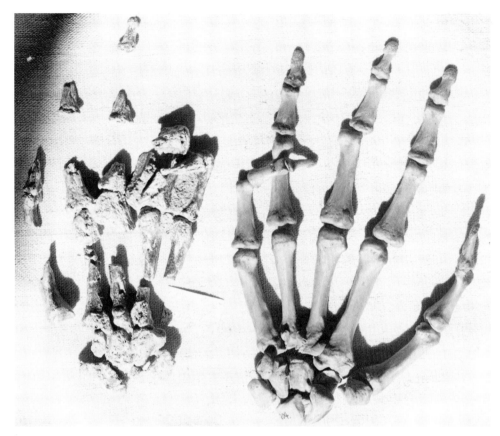

Figure 47. Palmar view of left hand (compared with right hand of modern, young, Black male [Terry #204]), showing development associated with strong finger extension. Dislocation of little finger probably post-mortem.

Morphology and Genetic Relations

We have already noted that the Wadi Kubbaniya man, with his wiry slender build with short trunk, long distal limb segments and linear but strong-faced, wide-nosed, prominent-jawed skull, would fit into the center of the range of variation of the Jebel Sahaba hunters. We will now consider this in detail.

Skull

The vault is quite low, fairly narrow and was probably long, either ovoid or byrsoid in top view (as indicated by the restoration of frontal and temporal bones). The frontal bone has a fairly narrow (pinched) but rather high (44 mm) and vertical (88°) forehead, and, as noted, extremely heavy divided browridges above an extremely deep nasion depression. It has no trace of metopic suture or of frontal neuro-vascular grooves. The temporal bone has an almost flat squama, probably a large mastoid process and wide-springing and thick (6 mm) zygomatic process (Figures 31 and 33).

The base shows a basi-occipital of smallish size (25 mm long) with prominent condyles, small pharyngeal fossa, but, together with the sphenoid, an adequate pituitary fossa ($11 \times 16 \times 8$ mm a-p×transv.×depth). Base breadth is average (118 mm biauricular) for a linear skull.

The face is wide, low and unexpectedly flat with nasion projecting only 19 mm from the zygo-frontal surface plane, and 11 mm from the bi-dacryal plane (Woo and Morant 1934). The cheek bones are massive, flaring and forward-placed (porion to infraorbitale radius of 80 mm is *ca*. 10 mm above average). Orbits are low and rectangular with extremely small (3°) droop from the horizontal. Nose is low and wide, as noted, with low root, low and wide bridge, small (?) and (pointed) spine and slight subnasal grooves. More striking is the prognathism

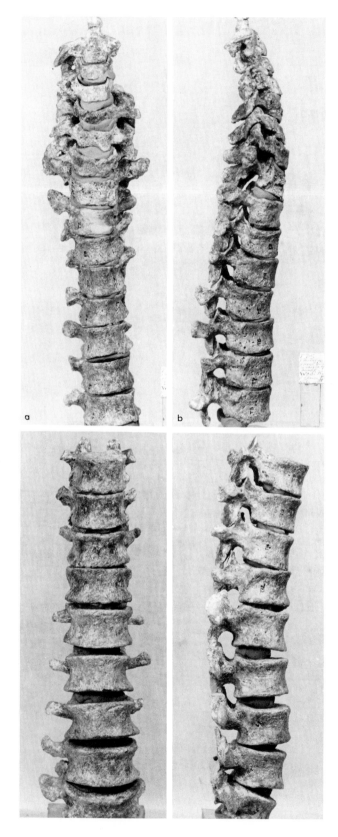

Figure 48. Vertebral column (front and right side).

Figure 49. Inferior surfaces of 3rd–5th lumbar vertebrae, showing extension stress in slight twin concavities in dorsal third of disk surfaces, like incipient Scheuermann's disease.

(gnathic index 108, profile angles 75° overall and 52° for upper alveolae) and non-projecting chin (106° with horizontal). The jaw, accurately restored by T.D.S., has square angles, fair muscularity and the slight inversion of posterior border of the ramus expected in Sub-Saharan Africans. Figure 53 shows comparison of the Kubbaniya specimen with Upper Paleolithic, modern Black and Australoid faces.

Postcranial Skeleton

Table 8 gives comparative data for post-cranial, male skeletons. The data from Jebel Sahaba, in Nubia, are from Anderson (1968) and Wendorf (1968a), those from Taforalt, in Morocco, are taken from Ferembach (1962) and those for the modern U.S. White and Black specimens were taken by J.L.A. and J.O.K. For the indices marked *, we have used Martin's technique (1928), except for skull base height, auricular-basion, for which J.L.A. has devised his own technique partly following G. Neumann and, earlier, Adolf Schultz. Dakryon is used for orbit breadth. Sitting height and shoulder breadth are determined by placing the bones in their positions in life. As can be seen in Table 8 and in previous comparisons, the linear, wiry, short-trunked, but fairly tall body build with long forearms (and shins) is identical to slightly later, Upper Paleolithic Nubians at Jebel Sahaba (Anderson 1968). It is also similar to that of other desert-adapted or even savannah-adapted populations of Upper Paleolithic to modern times in the range from Morocco and Egypt to the lake country of East Africa. Some of the North African groups (Ferembach 1962; Briggs 1955) are more massive and less linear, but the long forearms do occur there (Taforalt, cited in Table 8) and among prehistoric East Mediterraneans (Angel 1972a). These features also occur in many Sub-Saharan African

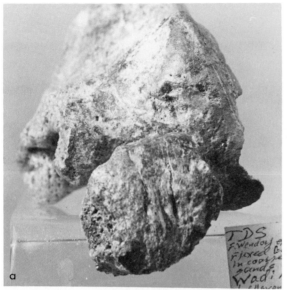

Figure 50. Signs of stress and trauma. a–Left patella shows broad vastus notch and smaller medial one; patellar surface of left femur shows strong lateral margin. b–Left distal tibia and anterior edge of trochlea and talus show slight ankle dorsiflexion facets (eroded post-mortem).

populations, but details of pelvis, scapulae and hands do not point to these latter populations.

General Comparisons

We have avoided the concepts and terms of White and Black, since the many populations making up these cultural or geographic entities today are widely variable. Each has a long microevolutionary history with considerable hybridization, temporary isolation, migration and change in population size. Hence, except as a method of standardization or as a reference for readers unfamiliar with prehistoric groups, it is not meaningful to compare the Wadi Kubbaniya specimen with modern U.S. Blacks and Whites as we have done in Tables 8 and 9 and in Figure 53. The proper comparisons would be with the hunting and fishing populations, between 20,000 and 8,000 B.P., along and beyond the Nile drainages, from the mountainous and forested terrain of Zaire to the savannah lake country, northward toward the Delta (actual Nile Delta sites obviously are very deeply buried), and finally with the chain of North African populations.

Whenever a chain of modern villages has been studied (Cyprus: Buxton 1920, Angel 1972b; Peru or Mexico: Lasker 1960; Melanesia: Oliver and Howells 1957; southeastern Turkey: Angel 1972a), it has been found that the rate of intermarriage between adjacent villages, usually 10–20% per generation, prevents sharp differences. However, there will be considerable differences between villages from opposite coasts of an island, or even from half a dozen villages apart in the valley. Also, these partly "inbred" villages often show such striking intra-family continuity and inter-family contrast that it is possible to assign an individual correctly to a given family through showing part of a complex of family traits. (This was not unknown in the past generation even in New England.)

From south to north in East Africa, such a chain of populations includes Ishango, Elmenteita, Gamble's Cave, Lothagam (cited in Angel *et al.* 1980), then a jump to Wadi Halfa (Greene and Armelagos 1972), Jebel Sahaba, then perhaps Badari (Morant 1935), Mechta, Afalou (Briggs 1955) and Taforalt (Ferembach 1962). (See Table 9; the data given there are from the same sources as were noted above for Table 8, with the addition of the data for the Mechta and Afalou skulls, taken from Briggs 1955.)

Along this long line of lakes, rivers, hills and seacoast, the very linear and quite low skull vault with sloping broad forehead extends north to Egypt, but becomes broader and higher, with more vertical but pinched or relatively narrow forehead, when we reach the northwest African sites. The extremely prognathous, wide, rather flat, broad-nosed, square-

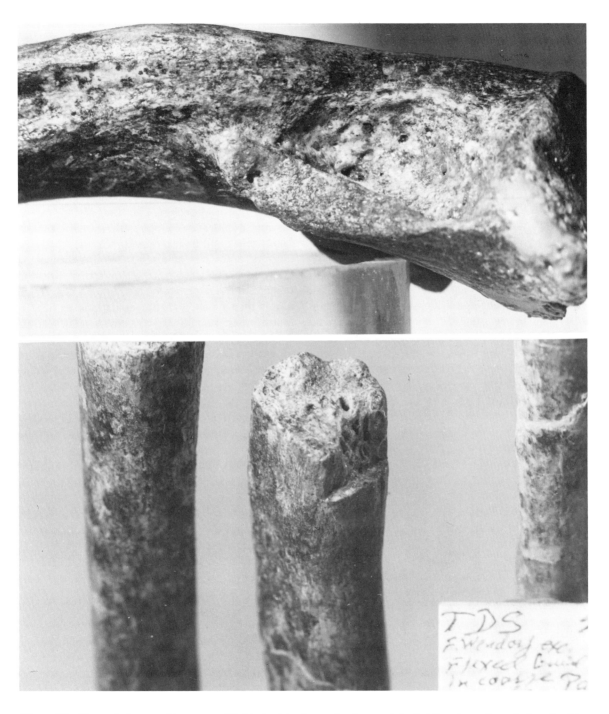

Figure 51. Signs of stress and trauma. a–Right clavicle shows development for holding-down force during shoulder action; b–right ulna shaft shows parry fracture healed 5–10 years before death.

Figure 52. Signs of stress and trauma. Upper end of extensor muscle crest of left humerus shows healing splinter of bone wedging chip of stone blade.

jawed and muscular face of the south-to-north East African sites changes considerably in the Maghreb to a much less prognathous, even squarer face, with much narrower and more prominent nose. Brow ridges remain very thick and strong over low and strikingly horizontal orbits throughout the south to north to northwest sequence. If we had Upper Paleolithic to early Mesolithic samples from Egypt, Libya and the northern Sahara, we would probably find a smooth transition from the Ishango-Lothagam-Elmenteita proto-Nilotics to the Mechta-Afalou proto-Moors and proto-Berbers. At present, however, this chain of populations is broken by the lack of information from the lower Nile and Libya.

Since this is the chain which is central to Coon's (1962, 1965) argument for a North Africa to the Cape proto-San "race" (Capoid), face flatness is also at issue. This is clearly not the Mongoloid or Australopith flatness of a huge face with very sloping chewing plane, in which massive cheek bones move forward for extra powerful masseter muscles and tend to leave behind a pinched forehead. Khoisan face flatness is a pulling back of the nose root in a smallish face with non-sloping chewing plane—the extreme of one African trend toward masseter exaggeration and the complete opposite of the Congo forest norm. This can occur in individuals in the chain of populations (there are examples at Lothagam, Wadi Kubbaniya, Taforalt and even in some Natufians), but it is not typical, neither is the vault-bossing, which occurs in Bushman-Boskop

and which is quite likely to be environmental (resulting from water-balance during lactation) rather than genetic. However, we would not yet completely discount Coon's interpretation, except that a southern origin seems unlikely.

We wish to avoid the double misconceptions between Greene and Armelagos (1976) and Rightmire (1970a, 1970b). Rightmire's stress on the marked variation of surviving San and their immediate skeletal ancestors is clear and correct. It is not at all to be expected that this group of populations should form a "type" that can be extended to East and North Africa: Greene and Armelagos (1976) are correct in this, but they may go too far in attacking the use of "types" as concepts. In any case, the realities are, on the one hand, genes and their direct growth effects (shovel incisors, or flatness of nose root, or inversion of jaw above gonial angles) and, on the other, breeding populations. Emphasis on the latter leads to the useful idea of a chain of populations in hunting times, which probably gave rise to a similar chain in farming times, even down to the present. In these terms the Wadi Kubbaniya, Jebel Sahaba and Wadi Halfa people are direct ancestors of modern Nubians, just as Lothagam Mesolithic fishermen are direct ancestors of the Turkana. It is wrong to see the prehistoric, the Pharaonic, Ptolemaic or modern Nubians as various kinds of White-Black hybrids; they have their own 18,000-year lineage.

We do not yet know what was there before the Upper Paleolithic. It could have been like the Near Eastern Neandertaloids, or the Ethiopian Omo River early *Homo sapiens* (Day 1969) directly transitional from the Kenyan *Homo erectus*, or still a third transitional form.

Summary

The Wadi Kubbaniya skeleton is a link in a chain of hunting and fishing peoples present in Africa, from 20,000 to 8,000 B.P. They are the direct ancestors of modern Nilotics, Nubians, Egyptians, probably Libyans and Berbers. This is the far-sighted, comparative view.

In themselves, the skull and skeleton are complete enough (after much work by T.D.S. and M.T.) to provide evidence of the appearance and way of life of the individual buried at Wadi Kubbaniya.

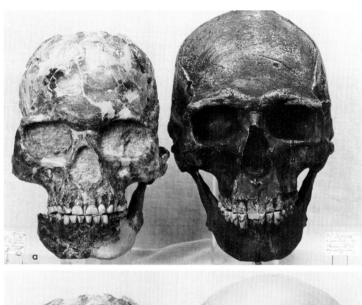

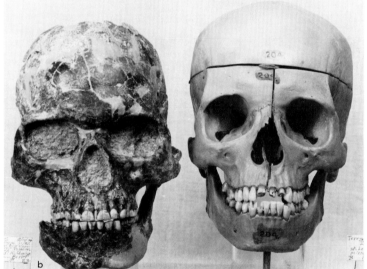

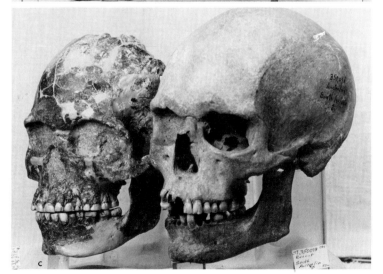

Figure 53. Comparison of Kubbaniya face with non-Africans. a–Predmost very similar for upper face and forehead; b–modern U.S. Black similar for lower nose, alveolar projection and chin; c–recent South Australian very similar except for Ialtu's nasal projection.

From shoulder, elbow, forearm and hand development, we know that he was a right-handed thrower and thruster (possibly of spears directed at game, fish and other humans) and skilled in the use of his hands, perhaps in making blades or nets. Back stress is present in the lumbar region, as incipient Scheuermann's disease, probably from early stress in the kill or transport of game and fish.

As earlier evidence from Jebel Sahaba (Wendorf 1968a) suggests, aggression and strife in the form of cranial and parry-fractures, plus projectile points embedded in bone, were definitely part of the local way of life, in contrast to the Northwest Africans. This young man had recovered from two injuries, a parry-fracture (at about age 15) and a left epicondylar wound (just healed), only to be felled in his early twenties by a spear in the back.

His skull base height, pelvis and teeth suggest good childhood nutrition. No hypoplasia is present, which would show seasonal deprivation, as in later hunting and agricultural groups. Only his stature is below average for hunting period standards, perhaps due to adolescent stress. There is no evidence for anaemia in the skull vault.

The face, which was relatively well-preserved because he was buried face down, looks "Australoid" in terms of modern racial variety. He was about 1.72 m in stature and of muscular but slender build, with a short trunk. In genetic morphology, he was prognathous, with low, broad nose and ramus (jaw) inversion. The sum of these traits places him near the Jebel Sahaba group, which was apparently directly ancestral to modern Nubians and Sudanese.

CHAPTER 5

CONCLUSION

by

Fred Wendorf and Romuald Schild

The Kubbaniya skeleton is essentially a surface find. When it was first discovered in 1982 it most closely resembled a block of stone. We ourselves had worked for two field seasons in Wadi Kubbaniya and had not realized that this block might have any special interest. The same is doubtless also true of the many people from the nearby village of Kubbaniya itself who must have passed near the stone. This difficulty in recognition contributed to the survival of the skeleton after its exposure on the surface. Once it had been recognized, however, the combination of detailed archaeological and geological field work and painstaking laboratory effort, extracted from this "block of rock" a significant amount of new knowledge concerning one of our least known periods of Egyptian prehistory. The best evidence we have indicates that the skeleton dates sometime before the period of the major Late Paleolithic occupation in Wadi Kubbaniya and after the development of Late Paleolithic bladelet technology in the Nile Valley. Thus the skeleton probably falls after 25,000 B.P., and perhaps after 30,000 B.P., and before 20,000 B.P.

DATING THE SKELETON

Although the precise age of the skeleton is not known, there are, nevertheless, several consistent lines of evidence, which provide a reasonably firm basis for determining when the burial might have occurred. This evidence includes the reconstruction of the sedimentary sequence in the vicinity of the burial, the degree of mineralization of the skeleton and the nature of the lithic artifacts found in direct association with the burial.

Reconstruction of the Sedimentary Sequence

The final phase of the complex sequence of Middle Paleolithic sediments, as they are preserved at the mouth of Wadi Kubbaniya, is the deposition of a coarse Sand Sheet around the margin of a small embayment at the edge of the floodplain. A sample of quartz sand from the Sand Sheet gave a thermoluminescence date of 89,000 B.P. ± 18,000 years (Gd-TL33). The skeleton is obviously more recent than this, because the burial pit had been cut into the Sand Sheet. After the deposition of the Sand Sheet, which presumably records a brief decline in the level of the Nile, the river rose to a level at least 4 m above the top of the Sand Sheet. Remnants of silts deposited during this period of higher Nile are preserved on the south side of Wadi Kubbaniya, but not in the area where the skeleton was found.

The level of the Nile then fell again, the exposed surface of the silts was eroded, and sand dunes filled deflated basins in the silts. It is not clear whether the dune accumulation occurred simultaneously with another rise in the level of the Nile, or if the dune merely filled hollows in the silt. Sand from the base of this dune gave a thermoluminescence date of 31,000 B.P. ± 8,000 years (Gd-TL32).

The next sedimentary event recorded at Wadi Kubbaniya is a rise in the level of the Nile so that the floods could once again enter the small embayment at the edge of the floodplain; at the same time, dunes began to accumulate in the embayment and around its margin. It is highly likely that the human burial precedes this event, because the fill of the burial pit consists entirely of coarse sand of the Sand Sheet with no traces of silt. Some silt would surely have been included when the grave was refilled had there been any present when it was dug. If we may conclude that no silt was present at that time, then the burial occurred either before these silts were deposited or after they were removed. In the latter case it would have been during the last few thousand years.

The rise in the level of the Nile and the deposition of the floodplain silts over and around the small embayment can be tied to two Late Paleolithic sites of the "Early Kubbaniyan" industry, located at the edge of the small embayment and about 120–150 m west of the burial. Charcoal from these two sites yielded four radiocarbon dates of 18,120 B.P. ± 670 years (SMU-1036), 18,360 B.P. ± 790 years (SMU-1129), 18,440 B.P. ± 690 years (SMU-1131) and 20,690 B.P. ± 280 years (SMU-1037). There are four additional radiocarbon dates from sites with closely similar lithic assemblages, located further up Wadi Kubbaniya, of 18,010 B.P. ± 340 years (SMU-1033), 19,340 B.P. ± 370 years (SMU-1033; second count on the same sample), 19,030 B.P. ± 180 years (SMU-1157), and 19,810 B.P. ± 310 years (SMU-1136). The dates cluster in two groups which might suggest two occupations separated by some 2,000 years; however, there is no evidence for this in either the archaeology or the stratigraphic setting. Instead, the younger group of dates (18,000–18,500 B.P.) is rejected as too recent because they conflict with strong stratigraphic evidence placing the up-wadi sites of this group before 18,500 B.P. It should also be noted that all but one of the younger dates have very large standard errors, suggesting a problem with either the size or nature of the sample. An age about 19,000–21,000 B.P. is indicated for all of the "Early Kubbaniyan" sites, including the two near the burial.

Nile floods, therefore, began to enter the small embayment and to cover over the burial site with silts at around 20,000–21,000 B.P. The level of the Nile continued to rise, with only a few minor pauses, until about 12,500 B.P. when it reached a level at least 10 m above the burial. By about 13,000 B.P. the mouth of Wadi Kubbaniya was choked by a mass of silts and sands so thick as to form a dam across the entire wadi, and seepage led to the formation of a huge lake behind this dam. Traces of the dam occur only 200 m up-wadi from the burial, and it is probable, although not demonstrable, that the riverfront slopes of the dam may have covered the burial site. In any case, the burial was deeply embedded, probably to a depth of several meters, within the Nile floodplain after 19,000 B.P. and was probably continuously saturated from that time until after 12,000 B.P., when the Nile fell rapidly to a level close to that of today. Evidence from other areas along the Nile suggests that after 10,000 B.P. the floods of the Nile were never again of sufficient height to reach the small embayment and the burial.

The early Holocene rains, which may have begun about 11,000 B.P., started to re-expose the small embayment and the burial site. At first, playas formed in the dry basin behind the dam which closed the wadi, but the run-off from the rains was soon

such that the dam was broken and the massive block of accumulated sands and silt began to be eroded, by water and later by wind. We cannot determine when the overlying blanket of interfingering silts and sands became so eroded as to expose the top of the Sand Sheet, but it is likely that this did not occur until fairly recently, perhaps after 5,000 B.P., when hyper-arid conditions and severe wind deflation prevailed.

Degree of Mineralization

It was the high degree of mineralization of the bones and the stone-like cementation of the block in which they were preserved that first suggested a significant antiquity for the skeleton. This degree of mineralization was very different from that observed for the numerous large and medium-sized mammal and fish bones in the Late Paleolithic sites in the vicinity of the skeleton and elsewhere in Wadi Kubbaniya. It also contrasted with the state of preservation of human remains from other Late Paleolithic sites along the Nile, such as Jebel Sahaba (Anderson 1968; Wendorf 1968a), Wadi Halfa (Greene and Armelagos 1972), Tushka (Wendorf 1968b), Esna (Butler 1974) and Nazlet Khater (Thoma 1984; Vermeersch *et al.* 1984a, 1984b).

The extreme mineralization of the Kubbaniya skeleton can probably be attributed to two factors. The first was what must have been the relatively loose fill of the grave pit compared to the surrounding laminated Sand Sheet. The second was the long period when the pit and the overlying sediments were saturated with water. These two combined to concentrate lime-rich water in the grave pit, which, when the water evaporated, became a massive concretion ultimately more indurated than the surrounding laminated Sand Sheet.

Thus, the degree of mineralization does not necessarily indicate that the human skeleton is significantly older than the unmineralized faunal remains found in the nearby Late Paleolithic settlements. Their different appearance can be readily explained as a result of the retention and concentration of water within the grave pit. The degree of mineralization of the skeleton, however, does indicate that the bones and the grave pit were subjected to a long period of saturation, and thus it is highly unlikely that the skeleton was placed in the pit after the Holocene re-exposure of the Sand Sheet, since no water covered the site after 12,000 B.P.

The condition of the lower limb fragments has been taken by Stewart and Tiffany to indicate either mutilation of the corpse or desecration of the grave by the human enemies of the individual buried there (see Chapter 4). However, we are skeptical of this interpretation. Throughout the Eastern Sahara, we have observed that when mineralized mammalian long bones become exposed on the surface, natural processes frequently lead to breakage both along and across the shaft, the several fragments then being reduced by aeolian action to rounded splinters and eventually to nothing. We see no reason why this could not have happened at Kubbaniya and feel no need to invoke extraordinary factors.

Associated Artifacts

The Mousteroid artifacts found in the Sand Sheet and on the deflated surfaces nearby are not pertinent to the age of the human skeleton, although they do provide an indication of when the Sand Sheet and the underlying sands and silts of the "Middle Paleolithic valley-filling event" were deposited. The two bladelets from opposed platform cores found with the skeleton are more relevant. Opposed platform bladelet technology was not known in Egypt prior to the Late Paleolithic, so the skeleton is not Middle Paleolithic in age. When the technology appeared is not known, but it is present at Nazlet Khater in the earliest dated Late Paleolithic from the Valley, between 30,000 and 33,000 B.P. (Vermeersch *et al.* 1982). The Nazlet Khater industry has not been described in detail, but it appears to contain numerous blades and bladelets with invasive retouch. There is no mention in the brief notes published thus far of Ouchtata bladelets in the assemblage. Their absence would suggest that they appeared after 30,000 B.P.; if so, then the Kubbaniya burial would date after that time.

Physical Type

Physical attributes suggest that the Kubbaniya skeleton can be grouped with the other Late Paleolithic remains from the Nile Valley which are generally classified as "Mechtoid" (Angel and Kelley, this volume). The Mechtoids were a population of primitive, robust *Homo sapiens* who occurred throughout North Africa from the Nile Valley to the Maghreb (Ferembach 1962). They are named after a series of skeletons excavated at the site of Mechta-el-Arbi in Algeria (Lagotola 1923; Cole 1928; Briggs 1950; Ferembach 1962). As far as is presently known, all of the skeletons of Late Paleolithic age from the Nile Valley are Mechtoids (Anderson 1968; Butler 1974; Greene and Armelagos 1972; Reed 1965; Thoma 1984), as are also those from the generally contemporaneous Ibero-maurusian sites in the Maghreb (Ferembach 1959, 1962; Briggs 1950; Ruhlmann 1951; Gobert and Vaufrey 1932; Arambourg *et al.* 1934). While there are minor differences in facial and mandibular structure among these populations, which seem to be localized specializations, the resemblances throughout this vast area are truly remarkable (Anderson 1968:1035).

In the Nile Valley, the Nazlet Khater skeleton is the oldest Mechtoid, if it can be associated with the nearby Late Paleolithic quarry which has several dates between 30,000 and 33,000 B.P. The Kubbaniya skeleton, which may best be dated as "older than 20,000 B.P.", would then be next in age. The two Esna skeletons are perhaps next; they have an associated radiocarbon date of about 16,000 B.P. but are probably two to three thousand years older, on the basis of the associated archaeology. The two large groups of skeletons from Jebel Sahaba and Wadi Halfa date to about 12,000–14,000 B.P., and the Kom Ombo frontal fragment is dated between 13,000 and 13,500 B.P. There are no burials known from the Nile Valley after 13,000 B.P. until well into the Holocene, by which time the Mechtoids were no longer present.

Cultural Factors

Burial Position

The Kubbaniya burial was placed in a long rectangular trench or pit, dug to an unknown depth into a coarse laminated sand sheet from a surface which has been destroyed by erosion. The body was placed in the pit face down, head to the east and arms to the side. The position of the legs is not known, but the position of the proximal portion of the right femur suggests that the legs were extended.

A face-down extended position is not common among Late Paleolithic burials, but it is not unknown. It was used on one of the Jebel Sahaba skeletons (Burial 29—Wendorf 1968b:873), although one leg of that burial was semi-flexed. The

Nazlet Khater burial was extended but face up (Vermeersch *et al.* 1984a:283), as were also three of the Wadi Halfa skeletons (Saxe 1966:6). The most frequent burial position for Late Paleolithic burials in the Nile Valley is on the side, with both the arms and legs flexed, hands to the face, and the heels of the feet against the base of the pelvis. There is no overall consistency in orientation, although on the left side with head to the east was preferred at Jebel Sahaba.

Burial Location

Two locations were favored for the placement of burials during the Late Paleolithic in the Nile Valley. At Wadi Halfa (Green and Armelagos 1972), Tushka (Wendorf 1968a) and Esna (Butler 1974), the bodies were placed in shallow pits in the occupation area. At Jebel Sahaba (Wendorf 1968b) and Nazlet Khater (Vermeersch *et al.* 1984a), on the other hand, the graves were placed in shallow pits on higher ground either above the settlement or nearby. (The village associated with the Sahaba graveyard was not located; it was assumed to have been at a slightly lower elevation and subsequently destroyed by erosion. Traces of a destroyed occupation of the appropriate age were present below the graveyard.) The use of ground above the village for the graveyard is also characteristic of Predynastic and later Egyptian periods. The Kubbaniya burial appears to be an isolated occurrence, with no evidence for a nearby contemporary settlement. As such, the burial is unique among the Late Paleolithic examples from the Nile Valley.

While there is no evidence of a Late Paleolithic village which might be associated with the Kubbaniya skeleton (those found are almost all associated with silts that are presumed to be later than the burial), it should be noted that the area between the burial and the river has been so extensively eroded that any traces of such a village would have been destroyed. Since it is likely that at the time of the burial the river was at a level somewhat lower than it

was at 20,000 B.P., a settlement could have been present nearby on or near what was then the floodplain. Thus, the isolation of the burial may be more apparent than real.

Evidence of Violence

An unusual feature of the Kubbaniya skeleton is the evidence of violence (Angel and Kelley, this volume). This consists of a healed parry fracture on the right ulna, more recent damage to the left humerus caused by a still embedded stone chip, and two bladelets in the abdominal cavity, one on the left side between the ribs and the lumbar vertebrae and the other against the second and third lumbar vertebrae. While there might be other possible explanations for the presence of the two bladelets in the abdominal cavity, the position of the body on its face (which would tend to inhibit the movement of objects into the body cavity) and the presence of the relatively fresh wound to the humerus strongly suggest that the most likely explanation is that they were part of a projectile which was lodged in the abdomen and caused the death of the individual.

Similar evidence of violence was noted on several of the bodies in the somewhat later Jebel Sahaba graveyard (Wendorf 1968a), where at least 40% of the individuals in the cemetery had died violently, independent of age and sex. It should be noted that the Nile at this time had a very limited and not very luxuriant floodplain, surrounded by an inhospitable, hyper-arid desert. There could well have been intense rivalry for this limited area, which rivalry occasionally led to violence.

We would hesitate to speculate that the same cause might have led to the death of the individual from Wadi Kubbaniya, but whatever the immediate cause of his death, the evidence from both Kubbaniya and Jebel Sahaba indicates that violence in human relations has considerable time depth. It did not appear with the onset of settled life in the Neolithic, but was present, at least in the Nile Valley, throughout much of the Late Paleolithic.

APPENDIX

DESCRIPTION OF SOME UPPER PLEISTOCENE SEDIMENTS FROM WADI KUBBANIYA, EGYPT

by

Christopher L. Hill and Romuald Schild

INTRODUCTION

As part of the interdisciplinary research effort into the prehistory of Wadi Kubbaniya, samples were collected from sediments associated with Upper Paleolithic archaeological occurrences, aeolian and fluvial deposits and lacustrine sequences in the wadi. This report gives a quantitative description of particle-size frequency-distributions of some Upper Pleistocene deposits in the Middle Paleolithic Area and Southern Section described elsewhere in this volume (Chapter 2).

Quantitative analysis and description of the grain-size distributions of sediments can be a useful method for attempting to discern correlations between specific depositional and post-depositional processes, or between paleoenvironmental settings and the characteristics of the sediment. Analyses of Kubbaniya samples were conducted primarily to evaluate the validity of the method as a means of describing sediments and, secondarily, to make comparisons within and between stratigraphic units.

SAMPLE COLLECTION AND ANALYSIS

The Kubbaniya samples were collected from selected trench and site profiles by Schild and Hill. Field descriptions of the sedimentary units and the collection of samples from Bore Hole 8/83 were by Schild. Particle-size analysis of all samples, except those from Bore Hole 8/83, was carried out at the Archaeometry Laboratory of the University of Minnesota, using a procedure specifically designed for microstratigraphic and archaeosedimentological studies (Gifford *et al.* 1982:66).

Gravel and sand-size fractions were wet sieved through a set of sieves ranging from -2.0 ϕ (4 mm) to 4.5 ϕ (0.044 mm) in 0.5 ϕ intervals. The silt and clay fractions were measured using the pipette procedure as described by Folk (1974). When only the gravel, sand, silt and clay-size fraction intervals were considered necessary, a modified wet-sieve

and pipette analysis was used, employing the gravel/sand (-2.0 ϕ) and sand/silt (4.0 ϕ or 0.062 mm) sieves, and then the pipette procedure to obtain the 4.0 ϕ and finer (total mud) and 8.0 ϕ (or 0.004 mm) and finer (total clay) size particles.

A computer program, modified from Slatt and Press (1976), generated some of the statistical parameters discussed in this report. The classification system follows Folk (1974). Textural classifications of the Lower Basin Silt, Lower Dune, Middle Basin Silt and Middle Dune Units were made using the data from Bore Hole 8/83, given above in Figure 14. For these units and for the samples described in Wendorf and Schild (1980: 25), sand:silt:clay ratios (to determine the percentage of the sample in each Wentworth class) were estimated using a slope intercept procedure on cumulative percentage curves.

SAMPLE LOCATION, CONTEXT, AND DESCRIPTION

The Late Quaternary sequence at Wadi Kubbaniya (Schild and Wendorf 1980, this volume) reflects a series of interrelated aeolian and fluvial events and consists, basically, of two sedimentary complexes (Figure A1). The older complex contains a series of six different dune and basin silt deposits and a floodplain silt; Middle Paleolithic occurs on the top of this sequence. The Upper Sand Sheet, which lies above the Lower, Middle and Upper Dunes and the Lower, Middle and Upper Basin Silts, has a date of 89,000 B.P. $\pm$ 18,000 years (Gd-TL33). In the Southern Section, the Floodplain Silts may be correlated with the silt deposits which interfinger with and overlie the Channel Sands and Silts. The Post-Middle Paleolithic Dune overlies the Middle Paleolithic Floodplain Silts and has been dated to 31,000 B.P. $\pm$ 8,000 years (Gd-TL32).

The younger sedimentary complex contains aeolian sediments interfingering with Nile silts and lacustrine deposits and dates from about 21,000 B.P.

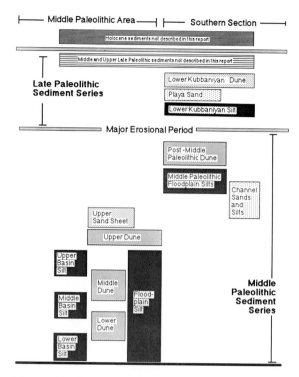

Figure A1. Schematic Late Quaternary stratigraphic sequence at Wadi Kubbaniya, with special reference to Middle and Late Paleolithic sediment complexes.

to 10,000 B.P. This complex includes the Lower Kubbaniyan Dune and the Lower Kubbaniyan Silt, as well as the lacustrine sands described in this report. The stratigraphic contexts, locations and gravel:sand:silt:clay histograms for the sediment samples analysed are given in Figure A2.

Floodplain Silt. The sample of the Floodplain Silt was obtained from Trench 8/82 where it is overlain by a dune. Here, the Floodplain Silt has a small blocky structure, is dark brown (10YR 4/3) and has slickensides and manganese stains. The sediment sample analysed from this unit contains about 7% sand, 30% silt and 63% clay. Texturally, it would be classified as clay.

Sediments from Bore Hole 8/83. Estimates of the textural classification of the Lower Basin Silt, Lower Dune, Middle Basin Silt and Middle Dune units were made using the data from Bore Hole 8/83 given in Figure 14. According to Folk's terminology (1974), the three samples from the Lower Basin Silt would be classified as sandy silt, with 15.5–48% sand, 40–61% silt and 12–23% clay.

The Lower Dune, above the Lower Basin Silt in Bore Hole 8/83, is composed of approximately 81% sand, 14–18% silt and <5% clay; texturally, it is a silty sand. A single sample of the Middle Basin Silt, which lies above the Lower Dune, is composed of about 57% sand, 41% silt and almost no clay; it would be classified as a silty sand. The three samples from the Middle Dune include 70–81% sand, 16–26% silt and <4% clay; the Middle Dune at Bore Hole 8/83 would be classified as a silty sand.

Upper Basin Silt. A sample of the Upper Basin Silt was taken from Trench 12/82, where it lies between the Middle and Upper Dunes. Here, the Upper Basin Silt exhibits a large blocky structure, has some slickensides and is pale brown (10YR 6/3); it contains patches of carbonates and is clearly mixed with the overlying sand. The sample contains approximately 10% sand, 25% silt and 65% clay, and would be defined texturally as a clay.

Upper Dune. Two samples of the Upper Dune were studied. One was from the Upper Dune above the Upper Basin Silt sampled at Trench 12/82, where it is structureless, consolidated and pale yellow (5Y 7/3); the other sample was taken from Trench 21/82, where the unit overlies the Floodplain Silts (Figure 15). The sample from Trench 12/82 is composed of >98% sand-sized grains, and would be texturally defined as a poorly sorted sand with near symmetrical skewness and a platykurtic graphic kurtosis. The sample from Trench 21/82 contains much less sand (*ca.* 12%), 6% silt and 83% clay, and would be called a sandy clay.

Upper Sand Sheet. A sample of the Upper Sand Sheet was taken from Trench 1/81 (Figure 9), where it is laminated, friable, very pale brown (10YR 7/3) and exhibits semi-rhythmic sorting of coarse-grained and medium-to-fine-grained, poorly sorted laminae. Platey carbonate lenses exist with the unit, which here overlies a truncated older dune. The sample contains <1% gravel, >94% sand and 4% clay; it is a poorly sorted gravelly sand, fine-skewed and platykurtic.

Channel Sands and Silts. A sample of the Channel Sands and Silts, representing alluvial Nilotic silts interfingering with the Middle Paleolithic floodplain silts, was taken near Site E-78-9. The sample is composed of about 3% sand, 81% silt and 16% clay; texturally, it is a silt.

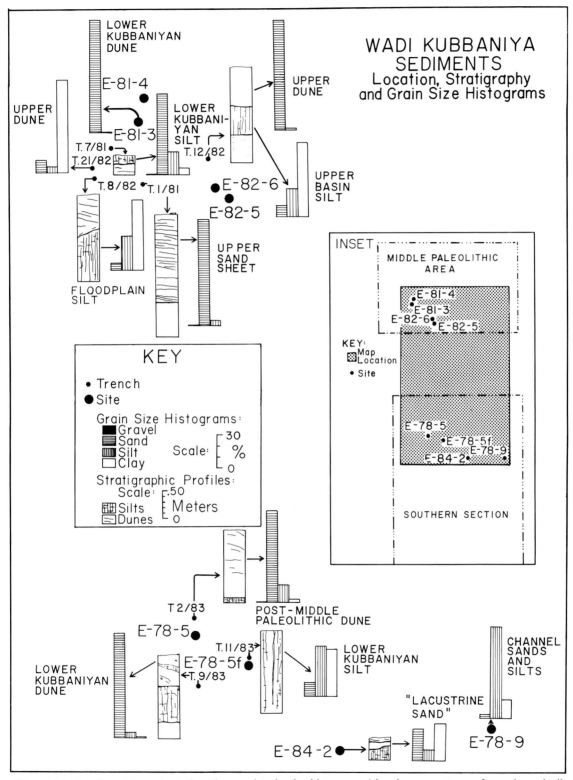

Figure A2. Stratigraphic contexts, locations and grain-size histograms (showing percentages of gravel, sand, silt and clay) for Late Quaternary sediments. Inset shows location of samples relative to Middle Paleolithic Area and Southern Section of Wadi Kubbaniya.

Post-Middle Paleolithic Dune. At Trench 2/83 near Site E-78-5, the Post-Middle Paleolithic Dune lies above the Floodplain Silt (Figure 20). The dune is loose to friable, bedded and very pale brown (10YR 8/3). Less than 1% of the sample is gravel, >80% is sand, about 16% is silt and 3% is clay; the sample would be designated as a poorly sorted, slightly gravelly, muddy sand. The skewness of the sample is near-symmetrical and the graphic kurtosis is mesokurtic.

Lower Kubbaniyan Silt. Two samples of the Lower (or Early) Kubbaniyan Silt were analysed, one from Trench 7/81 and one from Trench 11/83, near Site E-78-5f. At Trench 7/81, the cemented, light brownish grey (2.5YR 6/2) Lower Kubbaniyan Silt overlies a sand deposit (Figure 10). At Trench 11/83 (Figure 21), the Silt is a brown (7.5YR 5/2), thick (at least 1.6 m), massive vertisol with a medium blocky structure and large slickensides; pieces of charcoal, burned clay and isolated artifacts are embedded in it. The sample from Trench 7/81 is a very poorly sorted, slightly gravelly, muddy sand, containing <1% gravel, >72% sand, >20% silt and about 6% clay; it is strongly fine-skewed and has a mesokurtic graphic kurtosis. At Trench 11/83, the Lower Kubbaniyan Silt contains about 13% sand, 45% silt and 42% clay.

Lacustrine Sand. A sandy sediment lying above the Kubbaniyan Floodplain Silt at Site E-84-2 is considered to be a remnant of a small pond or playa deposit; a sample of it contains about 37% sand, 20% silt and 43% clay (or 63% mud). For comparison, sediments from two basins in the Isna area north of Wadi Kubbaniya (Wendorf and Schild 1976:62–79) appear to be more sandy than this sample: pond sediments from E71K14D are composed of about 74% sand and 23% mud, while those from E71K15 are about 82% sand and 18% mud. (Sand and mud percentages were derived from the intercept of cumulative curves and sand/mud boundaries using data given in Kossakowska-Such 1976: 327–329.)

Lower Kubbaniyan Dune. Two samples of the Lower Kubbaniyan Dune were analysed, one from Site E-81-3 and one from Trench 9/83 near Site E-78-5. The sample from Trench 9/83 (Figure 20) is from a loose, yellow (10YR 8/6), aeolian deposit containing silt lenses and *Bulinus* shells, which

overlies a unit correlated with the Lower Kubbaniyan Silt. It is composed of 93% sand, 5% silt and 1% clay, and is a moderately sorted, strongly fine-skewed, very leptokurtic sand. The sample from E-81-3 consists of 100% sand-sized particles and is moderately well-sorted, near-symmetrical and mesokurtic.

DISCUSSION

The techniques used to study the sediments from Wadi Kubbaniya provide an opportunity to evaluate the potential of particle-size frequency-distributions and the associated statistical parameters for comparisons within and between stratigraphic units and for determining paleoenvironmental conditions. A variety of factors can affect the final frequency distribution of particles in a specific sediment, including composition (mineralogy), source, depositional regime and post-depositional processes. Grain-size analysis is one method of studying these factors.

Discrimination of Stratigraphic Units

With the exception of the Lower Basin Silt (a sandy silt), all of the samples from Bore Hole 8/83 can be texturally classified as silty sands. The samples of the Lower and Middle Basin Silts contain at least 40% silt; however, clay-sized particles are estimated to form between 12% and 23% of the former sample, while the latter contains almost none. The samples of the Upper Basin Silt and Floodplain Silt contain >60% clay, >24% silt and 10% or less sand-size grains. They are both composed of at least 90% mud (silt+clay), and can be distinguished from the three samples of the Lower Basin Silt by having smaller amounts of sand and silt and greater amounts of clay. Compared to the Middle Basin Silt, the Upper Basin and the Floodplain Silts have at least 40% less sand, 10% less silt, and substantially more (>60%) clay. Although the sample of Floodplain Silt is slightly more sandy and clayey than the sample of the Upper Basin Silt, discrimination between these stratigraphic units based on only the percentages of sand, silt, and clay in the samples studied would not appear to be reliable.

Based on the ratio of sand, silt and clay (using the data from Bore Hole 8/83), it is not possible to discriminate reliably between the Lower Dune and Middle Dune.

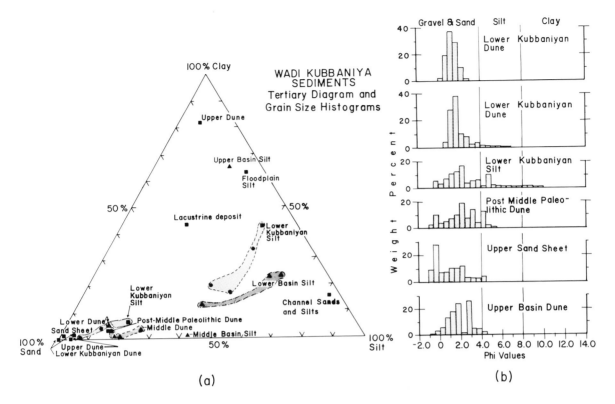

(a)   (b)

Figure A3. a–Relative frequencies of gravel+sand, silt and clay in selected sediments from Wadi Kubbaniya. KEY: squares–samples taken and studied by Hill; triangles–values for Bore Hole 8/83 derived from Figure 14; circles–data from Schild and Wendorf (1980:25); b–grain-size histograms for selected sediments.

The sample of Channel Sands and Silts contains >80% silt, almost no sand and about 16% clay. The negligible amount of sand distinguishes it from the Middle and Lower Basin Silts, where sand ranges from 15% to almost 60%, and from the aeolian-related deposits (Figure A3:a), while the high frequency of clay distinguishes it from the Upper Basin and Floodplain Silts.

On the basis of the grain-size analyses of Schild and Wendorf (1980) and data presented in this report, preliminary observations can be made concerning the variability within the Lower Kubbaniyan Silt. When the percentages of gravel+sand, silt, and clay are plotted on a tertiary diagram (Figure A3:a), the samples can be grouped into two sets. One includes three samples and is characterized by sand frequencies of >70% and clay frequencies of <10%. The other set contains four samples, characterized by 40% or less sand and higher frequencies of the silt and mud components. Such substantial differences between samples from what is considered to be one stratigraphic unit might indicate

different depositional facies within the deposit. They might also result from post-depositional processes, such as soil development within a particular stratum or differential weathering and the formation of clay-sized particles.

Depositional Environments

On the basis of field criteria, such as sedimentary structure and fossils, the sediments studied are considered to represent aeolian, river-channel, floodplain, basin and small lake or pond settings. Results obtained from the quantitative description of grain-size distributions indicate that certain textural characteristics are probably indicative of specific depositional environments. For example, some of the environments represented at Wadi Kubbaniya, such as the lacustrine sand above the Kubbaniyan Silt at Site E-84-2 and the Channel Sands and Silts near E-78-9, can apparently be distinguished on the basis of sand, silt and clay percentages alone

(Figure A3:a). However, it might be more difficult to use grain-size distributions to discriminate between basin and floodplain depositional environments, since similar sedimentary processes occur in both.

There are also difficulties when the grain-size distribution of a sediment appears to be complex, reflecting different types of sediment transport and depositional process. Single depositional environments might be inferred for unimodal grain-size distributions, as in the case of the Lower Kubbaniyan Dune samples (Figure A3:b). Sediments with polymodal distributions might reflect the presence of grains derived from more than one environmental situation. Variations in grain-size parameters might also be caused by the addition of post-depositional carbonates, organics, weathering products, or the mixing of sediments. The use of grain-size studies in conjunction with other sedimentological and mineralogical analyses is probably the most effective method of evaluating the paleoenvironmental and depositional settings.

In aeolian environments, sand dunes are generally characterized by good sorting and a skewness usually <1, caused by the absence of a coarse-grained tail in the particle-size distribution (Füchtbauer and Müller 1970, cited in Reineck and Singh 1975:119). The dune sands studied here range from moderately well and well sorted (the Lower Kubbaniyan Dune) to poorly sorted (the Post-Middle Paleolithic and Upper Dunes). Better sorting is a characteristic which is thought to distinguish aeolian sands from alluvial sands (Hassan 1985:59). Friedman (1961, 1967) was able to distinguish between fine-grained, unimodal, dune sands and beach and river-channel sands by the tendency of the dune sands to be fine-skewed (positive skewness). The aeolian samples from Wadi Kubbaniya are either nearly symmetrical or strongly fine-skewed (Figure A3:b).

In addition to being relatively well sorted, desert sands are usually fine to very fine and contain very little silt or clay (Blatt et al. 1980:645). The mean size range and grain-size histograms (Figure A3:b) indicate that these observations are generally true of the Kubbaniya aeolian samples. Aeolian-related sediments (except the Upper Dune sample from Trench 21/82, which is dominated by clay) are composed predominantly of sand-size grains, with almost no clay and very little silt. Median sizes range from 1.38 to 2.33 ϕ.

Compared to the samples considered representative of dunes, grain-size distributions from floodplain sediments appear to have sorting >2 and a skewness always <1 (Füchtbauer and Müller 1970). The analyses of the Lower Kubbaniyan Silt reflect these differences. It is more poorly sorted than any of the dune samples (2.31, or very poorly sorted) and more positively skewed (0.37, or strongly fine-skewed) than most of them. It also has a finer mean (2.71 ϕ) and median (2.28 ϕ) than any of the dune samples (means for the latter vary from 1.38 to 2.29 ϕ and medians from 1.38 to 2.33 ϕ) (Figure A3:b). Some of the samples from the Lower Kubbaniyan Silt contain high amounts of sand which might be derived from aeolian or higher-energy, fluvial environments (Figure A3:a, b). However, additional textural studies would probably be necessary to determine more precisely which geological processes are reflected in the grain-size distribution.

Compared with the representative dune samples and the Lower Kubbaniyan Silt, a sample of the Upper Sand Sheet has about the same sorting as most of the dune samples (0.95) but is different from the Silt; it is also fine-skewed (0.23), falling between the Silt and most of the dune sands. The Upper Sand Sheet sample has a mean size of 0.95 ϕ and a median size of 0.82 ϕ, and is coarser-grained than most of the dune samples.

CONCLUSION

The main purpose of the study of the particle-size frequency-distributions of sediments from Wadi Kubbaniya was to facilitate the description and comparison of stratigraphic units. Grain-size analysis can also be used to correlate lithologic units and help define depositional and post-depositional environments. Statistical parameters derived from the sediment particle-size distributions help to discriminate between and within stratigraphic units. When used with other textural (sphericity, roundness, surface textures) and mineralogical studies, information can be obtained about source, depositional settings and post-depositional processes. These and other types of geological studies can also be applied to the study of sediments from specifically archaeological contexts as well. The sedimentological study of lithostratigraphic units can thus help to evaluate more fully the environmental setting in which human activities took place.

REFERENCES

Adamson, D. A.
  1982 The integrated Nile. In *A Land Between Two Niles*, edited by M. A. J. Williams and D. A. Adamson. Rotterdam: Balkema. Pp. 221–234.

Adamson, D. A., R. Gillespie and M. A. J. Williams
  1982 Paleogeography of the Gezira and of the lower Blue and White Nile valleys. In *A Land Between Two Niles*, edited by M. A. J. Williams and D. A. Adamson. Rotterdam: Balkema. Pp. 165–219.

Allbrook, D.
  1961 The estimation of stature in British East African males. *Journal of Forensic Medicine*, Vol. 8, No. 1. Pp. 15–28.

Anderson, J. E.
  1968 Late Paleolithic skeletal remains from Nubia. In *The Prehistory of Nubia*, edited by F. Wendorf. Dallas: Fort Burgwin Research Center and Southern Methodist University Press. Pp. 996–1040.

Angel, J. L.
  1972a Biological relations of Egyptian and Eastern Mediterranean populations during pre-dynastic and dynastic times. *Journal of Human Evolution*, Vol. 2. Pp. 307–313.
  1972b Genetic and social factors in a Cypriote village. *Human Biology*, Vol. 44. Pp. 53–80.
  1980 Physical anthropology: determining sex, age, and individual features. In *Mummies, Disease and Ancient Cultures*, edited by M. Cockburn and E. Cockburn. Cambridge: Cambridge University Press. Pp. 241–257.
  1982 A new measure of growth efficiency: skull base height. *American Journal of Physical Anthropology*, Vol 58. Pp. 297–305.
  1984 Health as a crucial factor in the changes from hunting to developed farming in the Eastern Mediterranean. In *Paleopathology at the Origins of Agriculture*, edited by M. N. Cohen and G. J. Armelagos. Orlando: Academic Press. Pp. 51–73.

Angel, J. L. and J. O. Kelley
  1984 Experiment in human growth response to improving diet and disease control. *American Journal of Physical Anthropology*, Vol. 63. Pp. 63–134.

Angel, J. L., T. W. Phenice, L. H. Robbins and M. B. Lynch
  1980 Late stone-age fishermen of Lothagam, Kenya. *Michigan State University Anthropological Series 3*, No. 2. Pp. 141–201.

Arambourg, C., M. Boule, H. Vallois and R. Verneau
  1934 Les grottes paléolithiques des Béni Ségoual (Algérie). *Archives de l'Institut de Paléontologie Humaine*, 13. Paris.

Beaudet, G., P. Michel, D. Nahon, P. Oliva, J. Riser and A. Ruellan
  1976 Formes, formations superficielles et variations climatiques récentes du Sahara occidental. *Revue de Géographie Physique et Géologie Dynamique*, Vol. 18. Pp. 157–174.

Bisel, S. L. C.
  1980 *A pilot study in aspects of human nutrition in the ancient East Mediterranean, with particular attention to time universals in several populations from different time periods.* University of Minnesota: Ph.D. dissertation.

Blank, E. and S. Passarge
  1925 Die chemische Verwitterung in der ägyptischen Wüste. *Abhandlungen der Hamburger Univ. aus d. Gebiete d. Auslandkunde*, Vol. 17. Hamburg.

Blatt, H., G. Middleton and R. Murray
  1980 *Origin of Sedimentary Rocks.* New Jersey: Englewood Cliffs.

Briggs, L. C.
  1950 On three skulls from Mechta-el-Arbi, Algeria: a re-examination of Cole's adult series. *American Journal of Physical Anthropology*, Vol. 8. Pp. 305–13.
  1955 The Stone Age Races of Northwest Africa. *American School of Prehistoric Research, Peabody Museum Bulletin*, No. 18. Cambridge, Mass.: Harvard University.

Butler, B. H. (in J. E. Anderson)
  1968 The dentition (Late Paleolithic skeletal remains from Nubia). In *The Prehistory of Nubia*, edited by F. Wendorf. Dallas: Fort Burgwin Research Center and Southern Methodist University Press. Pp. 1018–1023.

Butler, B. H.
  1974 Skeletal remains from a Late Paleolithic site near Esna, Egypt. In The Fakhurian. A Late Paleolithic Industry from Upper Egypt, by D. Lubell. *Papers of the Geological Survey of Egypt*, No. 58. Cairo. Pp. 176–183.

Butzer, K. W.
  1970 Physical conditions in Eastern Europe, Western Asia and Egypt before the period of agricultural and urban settlement. In *Cambridge Ancient History Volume I*, edited by I. E. S. Edwards, G. J. Gold and N. G. L. Hammond. Cambridge: Cambridge University Press. Pp. 35–69.
  1980 Pleistocene history of the Nile Valley in Egypt and Lower Nubia. In *The Sahara and the Nile*, edited by M. A. J. Williams and H. Faure. Rotterdam: Balkema. Pp. 253–280.

Butzer, K. W. and C. L. Hansen
  1968 *Desert and River in Nubia: Geomorphology and Prehistoric Environments at the Aswan Reservoir.* Madison: University of Wisconsin Press.

Buxton, L. H. D.

1920   The anthropology of Cyprus. *Journal of the Royal Anthropological Institute,* Vol. 50. Pp. 183–235.

Chumakov, I. S.
1965   Pliocenovaia ingressia v dolinu Nila (po novym donnym). *Bull. Moskovskogo Obshtshevstva Ispit. Prirody, Novaia Seria, Otd. Geol.,* Vol. 40, No. 4. Pp. 111–112.
1967   Pliocenovyie i pleistocenovyie otlojenia doliny Nila w Nubii i Verhnem Egipte. *Transactions of the Geological Institute, Academy of Sciences of the U.S.S.R.,* Vol. 170. Moscow: Nauka.

Cole, F. A.
1928   Skeletal remains from Mechta-el-Arbi. *Logan Museum Bulletin,* Vol. 1, No. 2. Pp. 165–89.

Cook, D. C. and J. E. Buikstra
1979   Health and differential survival in prehistoric populations: prenatal dental defects. *American Journal of Physical Anthropology,* Vol. 51. Pp. 649–664.

Coon, C. S.
1962   *The Origin of Races.* New York: Knopf.
1965   *The Living Races of Man.* New York: Knopf.

Day, M. H.
1969   Early *Homo sapiens* remains from the Omo River region of southwest Ethiopia. *Nature,* Vol. 222. Pp. 1135–1138.

Ferembach, D.
1959   Les restes humains épipaléolithiques de la Grotte de Taforalt (Maroc oriental). *Comptes-rendus Hebdomadaires des Séances de l'Académie des Sciences,* Vol. 248. Pp. 3405–3467.
1962   *La Nécropole Epipaléolithique de Taforalt. Etude des Squelettes Humains.* Paris: Centre National de la Recherche Scientifique.

Folk, R. L.
1974   *Petrology of Sedimentary Rocks.* Austin: Hemphill.

Friedman, G. M.
1961   Distinction between dune, beach, and river sands from their textural characteristics. *Journal of Sedimentary Petrology.* Vol. 31. Pp. 514–529.
1967   Dynamic processes and statistical parameters compared for size frequency distribution of beach and river sand. *Journal of Sedimentary Petrology,* Vol 37. Pp. 327–354.

Füchtbauer, H. and G. Müller
1970   *Sediment-Petrologie. Teil II: Sedimente und Sedimentgesteine.* Stuttgart: Schweizerbartische.

Gasse, F.
1976   Interêt de l'étude des diatomées pour la reconstitution des paléoenvironnements lacustres. Example des lacs d'âge Holocène de l'Afar (Ethiopie et T.F.A.I.). *Revue de Géographie Physique et Géologie Dynamique,* Vol. 18. Pp. 199–216.

1980   Late Quaternary changes in lake-levels and diatom assemblages on the southeastern margins of the Sahara. *Palaeoecology of Africa,* Vol. 12. Pp. 333–350.

Gasse, F., P. Rognon and F. A. Street
1980   Quaternary history of the Afar and Ethiopian Rift lakes. In *The Sahara and the Nile,* edited by M. A. J. Williams and H. Faure. Rotterdam: Balkema. Pp. 361–400.

Gasse, F. and F. A. Street
1978   Late Quaternary lake-level fluctuations and environments of the northern Rift Valley and Afar region (Ethiopia and Djibouti). *Palaeogeography, Palaeoclimatology, Palaeoecology,* Vol. 24. Pp. 279–325.

Giegengack, R. F.
1968   *Late Pleistocene History of the Nile Valley in Egyptian Nubia,* Yale University, Ph.D. dissertation.

Gifford, J. A., G. Rapp Jr. and C. M. Moss
1982   The sedimentary matrix. In *Troy, the Archaeological Geology. Supplementary Monograph 4,* edited by G. Rapp Jr. and J. A. Gifford. New Jersey: Princeton University Press. Pp. 61–103.

Gobert, E. G. and R. Vaufrey
1932   Deux gisements extrêmes d'Ibéromaurusien. *L'Anthropologie,* Vol. 42. Pp. 449–490.

Greene, D. L.
1972   Dental anthropology of early Egypt and Nubia. *Journal of Human Evolution,* Vol. 1. Pp. 315–324.

Greene, D. L. and G. J. Armelagos
1972   The Wadi Halfa Mesolithic population. *Department of Anthropology Research Reports,* No. 11. Amherst: University of Massachusetts.
1976   The Wadi Halfa population and Rightmire's interpretation of Later Pleistocene man in Africa. *American Anthropologist,* Vol. 78. Pp. 98–100.

Harvey, T. J.
1976   *The Palaeolimnology of Lake Mobutu Sese Seko, Uganda-Zaire: The Last 28,000 Years.* Duke University: Ph.D. dissertation.

Hassan, F. A.
1976a   Heavy mineral analysis of some Pleistocene sediments in the Nile valley. In *Prehistory of the Nile Valley,* by F. Wendorf and R. Schild. New York: Academic Press. Pp. 331–338.
1976b   Heavy minerals and the evolution of the modern Nile. *Quaternary Research,* Vol. 6. Pp. 425–444.
1985   Fluvial systems and geoarchaeology in arid lands: with examples from North Africa, the Near East, and the American Southwest. In *Archaeological Sediments in Context,* edited by J. K. Stein and W. R. Farrand. Orono, Maine: Center for the Study of Early Man. Pp. 53–68.

de Heinzelin, J.
1968   Geological history of the Nile valley in Nubia. In *The Prehistory of Nubia*, edited by F. Wendorf. Dallas: Fort Burgwin Research Center and Southern Methodist University Press. Pp. 19–55.

Irwin, H. T., J. B. Wheat and L. F. Irwin
1968   University of Colorado Investigations of Paleolithic and Epipaleolithic Sites in the Sudan, Africa. *University of Utah Papers in Anthropology*, No. 90. Salt Lake City: University of Utah Press.

Issawi, B.
1983   Ancient rivers of the eastern Egyptian Desert. *Episodes*, No. 2. Pp. 3–6.

Issawi, B., M. Y. Hassan and R. Osman
1978   Geological studies in the area of Kom Ombo, Eastern Desert, Egypt. *Annals of the Geological Survey of Egypt*, Vol. 8. Pp. 187–235.

Issawi B. and M. el Hinnawi
1980   Contribution to the geology of the plain west of the Nile between Aswan and Kom Ombo. In *Loaves and Fishes: the Prehistory of Wadi Kubbaniya*, assembled by F. Wendorf, R. Schild, edited by A. E. Close. Dallas: Department of Anthropology, Institute for the Study of Earth and Man, Southern Methodist University. Pp. 311–330.

Kelley, J. O. and L. J. Angel
1983   The workers of Catoctin Furnace. *Maryland Archaeology*, Vol. 19. Pp. 2–17.

Kendall, R. L.
1969   An ecological history of the Lake Victoria Basin. *Ecological Monographs*, Vol. 39. Pp. 121–176.

Kennedy, K. A. R.
1983   Morphological variations in ulnar suppinator crests and fossae as identifying workers of occupational stress. *Journal of Forensic Sciences*, Vol. 28. Pp. 871–876.

Kossakowska-Such, J.
1973   Analysis of grain from Sites E71K14 and E71K15. In *Prehistory of the Nile Valley*, by F. Wendorf and R. Schild. New York: Academic Press. Pp. 327–329.

Lagotola, H.
1923   Etude des ossements humains de Mechta-el-Arbi. *Recordes des Notices et Mémoires de la Société Archéologique du Département de Constantine*, Vol. 55. Pp. 145–176.

Lasker, G. W.
1960   Variances of bodily measurements in the offspring of natives and of immigrants to three Peruvian towns. *American Journal of Physical Anthropology*, Vol. 18. Pp. 257–261.

Marks, A. E.
1968   The Khormusan industry. In *The Prehistory of Nubia*, edited by F. Wendorf. Dallas: Fort Burgwin Research Center and Southern Methodist University Press. Pp. 315–391.

Martin, R.
1928   *Lehrbuch der Anthropologie*. Stuttgart: Fischer.

McKern, T. W. and T. D. Stewart
1957   *Skeletal Age Changes in Young American Males*. Technical Report EP-45 of the Headquarters Quartermaster Research and Developmental Command, Nantick, Mass.

Morant, G. M.
1935   A study of predynastic Egyptian skulls from Badari, based on measurements taken by Miss B. N. Stoessiger and Professor D. E. Derry. *Biometrika*, Vol. 28. Pp. 293–308.

Oliver, D. L. and W. Howells
1957   Micro-evolution: cultural elements in physical variation. *American Anthropology*, Vol 59. Pp. 965–978.

Reed, C. A.
1965   A human frontal bone from the Late Pleistocene of the Kom Ombo Plain, Upper Egypt. *Man*, Vol. 95. Pp. 101–104.

Reineck, H. E. and I. B. Singh
1975   *Depositional Sedimentary Environments, with Reference to Terrigenous Clastics*. New York: Springer.

Rightmire, G. P.
1970a   Iron Age skulls from southern Africa reassessed by multiple discriminant analysis. *American Journal of Physical Anthropology*, Vol. 33. Pp. 147–168.
1970b   Bushman, Hottentot and South African Negro crania studied by distance and discrimination. *American Journal of Physical Anthropology*, Vol. 33. Pp. 169–196.

Rognon, P.
1980   Une extension des déserts (Sahara et Moyen Orient) au cours du Tardiglaciaire (18,000–10,000 B.P.). *Revue de Géologie Dynamique et de Géographie Physique*, Vol. 22. Pp. 313–328.

Rognon, P. and M. A. J. Williams
1977   Late Quaternary climatic changes in Australia and North Africa: a preliminary interpretation. *Palaeogeography, Palaeoclimatology and Palaeoecology*, Vol. 21. Pp. 285–327.

Ruhlmann, A.
1951   La Grotte Préhistorique de Dar es Soltan. *Hésperis* II.

Said, R.
1962   *The Geology of Egypt*. Amsterdam: Elsevier.
1975   The geological evolution of the River Nile. In *Problems in Prehistory: North Africa and the Levant*, edited by F. Wendorf and A. E. Marks. Dallas: Southern Methodist University Press. Pp. 1–44.

1981   *The Geological Evolution of the River Nile.* New York: Springer.

Saxe, A. A.
   1966   *Social dimensions of mortuary practices in a Mesolithic population from Wadi Halfa, Sudan.* Paper prepared for the Annual Meeting of the American Anthropological Association.

Schild, R. and F. Wendorf
   1980   The Late Pleistocene lithostratigraphy and environment of Wadi Kubbaniya. In *Loaves and Fishes: the Prehistory of Wadi Kubbaniya*, assembled by F. Wendorf, R. Schild, edited by A. E. Close. Dallas: Department of Anthropology, Institute for the Study of Earth and Man, Southern Methodist University. Pp. 11–47.

Shukri, N. M.
   1950   The mineralogy of some Nile sediments. *Quarterly Journal of the Geological Society, London*, Vol. 105 and 106. Pp. 511–534 and 466–467.
   1951   Mineral analysis tables of some Nile sediments. *Bulletin of the Desert Institute*, Vol. 1. Pp. 10–67.

Shukri, N. M. and N. Azer
   1952   The mineralogy of Pliocene and more recent sediments in the Fayum. *Bulletin of the Desert Institute*, Vol. 2. Pp. 10–53.

Sillen, A. and M. Cavanaugh
   1982   Strontium and paleodietary research: a review. *Yearbook of Physical Anthropology*, Vol. 25. Pp. 67–90.

Sillen, A. and P. Smith
   1984   Weaning patterns as reflected in strontium-calcium ratios of juvenile skeletons. *Journal of Archaeological Science*, Vol. 11. Pp. 237–245.

Singleton, W. L. and A. E. Close
   1980   Report on Site E-78-11. In *Loaves and Fishes: the Prehistory of Wadi Kubbaniya*, assembled by F. Wendorf, R. Schild, edited by A. E. Close, Dallas: Department of Anthropology, Institute for the Study of Earth and Man, Southern Methodist University. Pp. 229–244.

Slatt, R. M. and D. E. Press
   1976   Computer program for presentation of grain size data by the graphic method. *Sedimentology*, Vol. 23. Pp. 121–131.

Stewart. T. D.
   1976   Evidence of handedness in the bony shoulder joint. *American Academy of Forensic Sciences, Abstracts of Annual Meeting.* (Washington, D.C.)
   1979   Handedness. In *Essentials of Forensic Anthropology*. Springfield, Ill.: Thomas. Pp. 239–244.

Street, F. A. and A. T. Grove
   1979   Global maps of lake-level fluctuations since 30,000 yr. B.P. *Quaternary Review*, Vol. 12. Pp. 83–118.

Thoma, A.
   1984   Morphology and affinities of the Nazlet Khater man. *Journal of Human Evolution*, Vol. 13. Pp. 287–296.

Trotter, M. and G. C. Gleser
   1958   A re-evaluation of estimation of stature based on measurements of stature taken during life and of long bones after death. *American Journal of Physical Anthropology*, Vol. 16. Pp. 79–124.

Uhden, R.
   1929   Der libysche Ur-Nil in Oberägypten. *Geologische Rundschau*, Vol. 20.

Vermeersch, P. M., M. Otte, E. Gilot, E. Paulissen, G. Gijselings and D. Drappier
   1982   Blade technology in the Egyptian Nile Valley: some new evidence. *Science*, Vol. 216. Pp. 626–628.

Vermeersch, P. M., G. Gijselings and E. Paulissen
   1984a   Discovery of the Nazlet Khater man, Upper Egypt. *Journal of Human Evolution*, Vol. 13. Pp. 281–286.

Vermeersch, P. M., E. Paulissen, G. Gijselings, M. Otte, A. Thoma, P. van Peer and R. Lauwers
   1984b   33,000-year old chert mining site and related *Homo* in the Egyptian Nile Valley. *Nature*, Vol. 309. Pp. 342–344.

Wendorf, F. (ed.)
   1968   *The Prehistory of Nubia.* Dallas: Fort Burgwin Research Center and Southern Methodist University Press.

Wendorf, F.
   1968a   Site 117: a Nubian Final Paleolithic graveyard near Jebel Sahaba, Sudan. In *The Prehistory of Nubia*, edited by F. Wendorf. Dallas: Fort Burgwin Research Center and Southern Methodist University Press. Pp. 954–995.
   1968b   The cultural materials at Site 8905. In *The Prehistory of Nubia*, edited by F. Wendorf. Dallas: Fort Burgwin Research Center and Southern Methodist University Press. Pp. 864–940.

Wendorf, F. and R. Schild
   1976   *Prehistory of the Nile Valley.* New York: Academic Press.
   1980   *Prehistory of the Eastern Sahara.* New York: Academic Press.

Wendorf, F., R. Schild (Assemblers) and A. E. Close (Editor)
   1980   *Loaves and Fishes: the Prehistory of Wadi Kubbaniya.* Dallas: Department of Anthropology, Institute for the Study of Earth and Man, Southern Methodist University.

Wendorf, F., R. Schild, A. E. Close, D. J. Donahue, A. J. T. Jull, T. H. Zabel, H. Wieckowska, M. Kobusiesicz, B. Issawi and N. el Hadidi
   1984   New radiocarbon dates on the cereals from Wadi Kubbaniya. *Science*, Vol. 225. Pp. 645–646.

Wendorf, F., R. Schild and H. Haas
   1979   A new radiocarbon chronology for prehistoric sites in Nubia. *Journal of Field Archaeology*, Vol. 6. Pp. 219–223.
Williams, M. A. J. and D. A. Adamson
   1974   Late Pleistocene desiccation along the White Nile. *Nature*, Vol. 248. Pp. 584–586.
Woo, T. L. and G. M. Morant
   1934   A biometric study of the "Flatness" of the facial skeleton in man. *Biometrika*, Vol. 26. Pp.

196–250.
Yesner, D. R.
   1980   Nutrition and cultural evolution. In *Patterns in Prehistory*, edited by N. W. Jerome, R. F. Kandel, and G. H. Pelto. Pleasantville, N.Y.: Redgrave.
van Zinderen Bakker Sr., E. M.
   1972   Late Quaternary lacustrine phases in the southern Sahara and East Africa. *Palaeoecology of Africa*, Vol. 6. Pp. 15–27.